AQUA / TERRA

REFLECTIONS ON THE WORLD OCEAN

Peter Neill

World Ocean Observatory

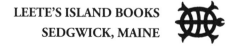

LEETE'S ISLAND BOOKS
SEDGWICK, MAINE

Leete's Island Books
Post Office Box 1 Sedgwick, Maine 04676

Libray of Congress Number 2020918267
ISBN 978-0-918172-84-6 (paper)
ISBN 978-0-918172-85-3 (epub)

First Edition
LeetesIslandBooks.com
in association with World Ocean Publications
World Ocean Observatory
worldoceanobservatory.org

Cover art by Mary Barnes
marybarnesart.com
Painting: *Barometric Low*
15 X 15, oil on canvas

Cover and book design by Trisha Badger
Printed by Penmor Lithographers, Lewiston, Maine

Other titles by Peter Neill

Non-Fiction:

*The Once and Future Ocean: Notes Toward
a New Hydraulic Society* (2016)
On a Painted Ocean (1998)
Great Maritime Museums of the World (1991)
Maritime America (1988)

Fiction:

3 (2014)
Acoma (1978)
Mock Turtle Soup (1972)
A Time Piece (1970)

Anthologies:

American Sea Writing (2000)
The City: American Experience (1978)

For Mary: Mermaid

I do not know what I may appear to the world; but to myself I seem to have been only like a boy playing on the seashore, and diverting myself in now and then finding a smoother pebble or a prettier shell than ordinary, whilst the great ocean of truth lay all undiscovered around me.

- Sir Isaac Newton (1642 - 1727)

INTRODUCTION

In my book *The Once and Future Ocean – Notes Toward a New Hydraulic Society*, I proposed a new paradigm for the 21st century, a framework for managed growth in the name of sustainability and driven by the ocean/freshwater continuum, a context for change that could transform many aspects of life beginning immediately from the bottom up, inside out, with no procrastinating need for massive investment or technological innovation. It was both a journalistic and political endeavor, analyzing the state of the ocean through multiple perspectives and offering an alternative vision to replace the bankrupt conventions and institutions that have so devastated the earth, the air, and, soon enough to come, the sea.

Its reception was modest, some welcome, some recognition of prescience and possibility, both mostly quiet immersion as if the vision was floating out there in an ephemeral future, its practicality uncertain, or least requiring more energy and engagement than seemed possible in the social and political reality of 2016 and after. While I am not a visionary, I do assert that "hydraulic society" is a vision for the future that is not only possible, but probable, perhaps inevitable, given the continuing over-use, commodification, privatization, pollution, conflict, and exhaustion of the world water supply without which no individual, family, community, or nation-state can survive.

My frustration is grounded in the obvious tragedy of this loss foretold. There are so many examples of water disruption as a result of drought, irresponsible demand, financial inequity, and political conflict that it seems evident to me that without some understanding of this critical, existential problem, any other vision or strategy will inevitably fail. No matter how novel and technological our responses, we will simply not succeed without adequate, sustaining water.

The ocean will be the only available source of supply. The ocean will provide when the aquifers, watersheds, and riverine systems are corrupted and depleted. The ocean will be the source of our drinking water, our food, our medicine and public health, our energy, our therapy, and our community. Land, no longer arable, will continue the existing migration from dry centers to livable coasts, transformed and protected from storm and sea level rise as concentrated centers for work and play. The world will affirm that water, as the most fundamental human right, the judicious harvest, management, and distribution of which will be the organizing principle by which 21st century society will survive.

I continue to search for the tools of persuasion. One such is the World Ocean Observatory (W2O), an on-line place of exchange for information and educational services about the ocean defined as "an integrated, global, social system," thus transcending conventional focus on species and habitat relating the ocean to every aspect of human endeavor. W2O advocates through responsible science and compelling cultural example, using communication platforms enabled by new pathways to access and engagement via the Internet. While it reaches millions worldwide, it, too, is not enough to foment the interest and action required to meet the impending challenge.

In my reading, I find that I often respond best to persuasion over polemic, and the literature of the environmental movement includes brilliant examples of such quiet observations, closely held, emotionally felt and expressed, that have invaded our barriers of rationality and schooled resistance to affect a subtle shift, a first wave of insight, an expansion of realization, and an impetus for shifting awareness, innovative thinking, and progressive involvement. Such texts frequently mimic the forms of Nature, meandering like a stream, aggregating like a pond or lake, and descending into the psyche as a repeating force for re-vision and re-dedication.

If you accept this idea of riverine passage, then the structure of this small book shows an organization from Confrontation to Connection to Revolution to Reflection. It begins at the intersection of land and sea, flows on to examples of oceanic inter-connection, circulates in a gyre of revolutionary proposals, and ends in a pool of reflections where facets of the ocean appear in association with my personal feelings and observations.

There is no argument made here. What follows are brief essays and insights that relate to an individual understanding of actuality and possibility. I hope you will respond with the same spirit with which they are offered: each of us is finding an individual way. If we meet alongshore or at sea hereafter, perhaps we can share our thoughts about these and other matters that unite us all in the great encompassing ocean world where we all swim together, mindful and generous and connected.

If I can hope for one positive outcome from your reading, I would wish that you are inspired to transform each of the nouns of this thematic passage into verbs:

Confront. Connect. Revolve. Reflect.

In such connected, determined action lies the nascent power of a global community of Citizens of the Ocean, a force as deep, wide, and dynamic as the ocean itself.

CONFRONTATION

AQUA / TERRA

CONFRONTATION

THE HARD EDGE

Our traditional approach to potential inundation by water has been the hard edge. It represents our cultural assumption that Nature is there to serve our needs and, when we think necessary, be engineered to that advantage. You see hard edges everywhere. Sea walls. Dikes and levees. Riprap erosion controls. Dams. Canals that artificially connect water bodies for transport by ship, for hydropower, or for redirection away from alternative, more economically desirable development.

Indeed, we have created large bureaucracies – the Army Corps of Engineers in the United States, for example – with the mission to protect us from the encroachment of water, to shield ports and harbors against storm and surge, to facilitate the most efficient marine transportation, and to otherwise manage the environment, lakes, inland waterways, and coasts to human advantage as defined by the financial exigencies of the time.

The fate of coastal wetlands is a blatant example of hard over soft. Once serving as massive buffers against storm incursion, wetlands served human needs additionally through complementary cultivation of hay for salt-water farms. But as those farms gave way to more concentrated settlement and sprawl, the marshes were first ditched to control pesky mosquitoes, a disruption of the natural arrangement that increased erosion and drained the buffer zone, followed by hard edges behind which were deposited dredge spoils, construction debris, and other unnatural material that transformed the soft soil into hard ground, on which is constructed more housing, parking lots, shopping malls, and manufacturing plants – all uses antithetical to Nature. You could describe a similar history for the destruction of coastal mangroves in other areas around the world.

Highways are hard edges. In southern New England where I once lived, the major north-south interstate highway, which extends from Florida to Maine, was built to follow a coastal route: it created a concrete wall between the shore and the entire land mass and marine system upstream to the point that the whole natural watershed was blocked and re-directed to a series of cement conduits beneath the highway. This blockage interrupted and concentrated the natural drainage, as well as the animal migration and surface water distribution that sustained the historical ecosystem, resulting in all sorts of changes, disruptions, and negative environmental consequences to the region.

More modern examples of hard edge thinking include such things as the Thames Barrier designed to protect London, England, from flooding. The structure is built across a 1,710-foot-wide stretch of the Thames, dividing the river into four 200-foot and two 100-foot navigable spans. There are also four smaller non-navigable channels between nine concrete piers and two abutments. The floodgates across the openings are circular segments in cross section that operate by rotating, raised to allow "under spill" for operators to control upstream levels and a complete 180-degree rotation for maintenance. All the gates are hollow and made of steel up to 1.6 inches thick. The gates fill with water when submerged and empty as they emerge from the river. The four large central gates are 66 feet high and weigh 3,700 tons. Four radial gates by the riverbanks, also about 100 feet wide, can be lowered. These gate openings, unlike the main six, are non-navigable. In a January 2013 letter to The London Times, a former member of the Thames Barrier Project Management Team, Dr. Richard Bloore, stated that the flood barrier was not designed with increased storm and sea level rise in mind, and called for a new barrier to be explored immediately.

On the continent, the Netherlands has long used a hard edge to protect the almost two-thirds of its national territory that is at or below sea level and otherwise susceptible to flooding by three major rivers: the Rhine, Meuse, and Scheldt. Before 1000 AD, the Dutch began to protect their coastal areas with earthen dykes, followed by timber walls, then by taller structures reinforced by crushed rock and cement, covered over by earth on which sheep continue to graze. But flood control engineering was soon augmented by the need for increased protection and the Dutch innovated radically with the construction of an enormous barrier system that closed the natural opening to the ocean and transformed the Zuiderzee into the IJsselmeer – literally, a sea to a lake. This was followed in the 1990s by the Delta Works, an even larger storm surge protection system already considered inadequate for projected sea level rise, sending Dutch engineers back to the drawing board.

THE SOFT EDGE

Some years ago, a museum exhibit comparing American and Norwegian maritime cultures provided an understanding of how to respond successfully to the challenges of the ocean with two very different solutions. In this case, it was boat construction. Traditional Norwegian boats are made with light ribs and planks that flex and conform visibly to the shifts in wave and water condition. By contrast, traditional American boats were built with planks on rigid frames and, while no less adaptive, these vessels confronted the ocean differently: they ride on the wave, rather than in, allowing them to push over or through the water rather than adapt to the forces in play.

The contrast may be extended to ideas of how to protect ourselves and property from storm and sea level rise. "Hard edges," referring to the use of dikes and sea walls, dams and sea gates as barriers to the ocean, is a fortress concept that engineers a didactic structural response to inundation using earthen bulwarks, cement walls, and giant doors that can be closed against the marauding sea. But what if there is another way?

The obvious alternative is "soft edges," more amorphous and flexible ways to absorb rather than divert the ocean's powerful incursions, indeed, to let the water in. This argument has been made often by environmentalists when opposing the filling in of wetlands, the destruction of marshes and coastal waterways, and the eradication of mangrove forests that, for centuries, provided natural protection by embracing the water and its destructive power. We have seen the failure of hard edges as storms overwhelm barriers, destroy the resorts and beachfront homes, and otherwise demonstrate the hydraulic power of the ocean twice: once on the way in, and again on the way out as the water withdraws, doubling the destruction. We have only to look at the devastation at the wasted nuclear facility in Fukushima, Japan, to witness this two-part threat.

There are emerging examples of soft edge response, exacerbated by the undeniable rise in sea level in many places, the consequent frequent flooding, and the unmitigated results of ever-increasing incidence of more powerful storms like Superstorm Sandy in the US in 2012. How can we turn these new circumstances to advantage?

In the Netherlands, long the most successful proponent of hard edge strategy, government is now evicting farmers from polders or marshes enclosed by dykes and converted to agriculture to restore those places as containment areas when the other defenses are overwhelmed. According to a New York Times report, the Dutch have expanded this concept to a $3 billion integrated plan to construct and connect flood controls, spillways, polders, smaller dykes, and pumping stations, forming an engineered capillary system that can accommodate vast increases in flooding volume as an alternative to public investment in additional and very expensive hard edge security.

There are other examples of this evolving thinking. After Hurricane Sandy, Governor Andrew Cuomo of New York proposed that coastal properties susceptible to continuous flooding be purchased by government, that the owners be compensated and relocated, and that the land be designated for public recreation and as natural barriers to future storm events. The cost benefit analysis of the purchase and redefinition of coastal lands compares advantageously with the financial requirements of a single storm, not to mention those to follow, as a practical and economical allocation of taxpayer funding. Ironically, as the US Congress debated the allocation of public monies to reimburse Sandy-devastated coastal dwellers and businesses through reparation payments and a subsidized national insurance scheme that enables owners to rebuild where is, and sometimes as was, that very same federal program was advertising on television to recruit new clients for more coverage in those marginal areas. It made no sense. The cancellation of such an ill-advised insurance program would disable coastal development substantially in the US – a radical and necessary policy shift.

In other countries, private groups, supported by international NGOs, are initiating the restoration and replanting of extensive mangrove forests in coastal areas for the same reason: to rebuild a natural, relatively inexpensive system that has proven its effectiveness as both storm and habitat protection, a very different response based on knowledge and experience of Nature. In Arcata, California, city managers have created a wastewater treatment plant that passes effluence through a primary clarifier that separates suspended solids by means of a digester that transforms material into methane and compost for sale. The resultant fluids are sent to oxidation ponds and treatment wetlands for additional settling, and then to enhancement and treatment marshes (which also serve as recreation areas), and, ultimately, as clean water into Humboldt Bay – a natural hydraulic progress that mimics the natural cycle with effective result. It is this wisdom that we must look to for instruction lest we drown in our conventional thinking. It is through learning that we will find our way to new ideas for ocean solutions.

THE WORKING EDGE

When we speak about the ocean edge, we are discussing that circumferential line that delineates the terrestrial coasts, forming the invisible linear confrontation and connection between land and sea. We have characterized the identity of those boundaries as "hard" and "soft," and seen engineered and social responses that are at once examples of mitigation of – or adaptation to – the dynamic circumstance of proximate earth and water.

We can also present the edge thematically, as the amalgam of coherent activities that reflect both the real and symbolic implication of what takes place there as context for social behavior, organizational structure, and expression of value as both personal and communal in any given alongshore place or time.

Let's start with "the working coast." Historically, the distribution of settlement was drawn to natural harbors and shores where fishing and trade could be practiced in support of the people who lived there. This holds true for inland waters as well – the distribution of interior cities in similar locations connect up- or down-stream to the ocean outlets. The working coast was at first a secure place where a small boat could be dragged ashore, built and repaired, and re-launched as a means of harvest comparable to that of the land.

As vessels got larger on the early American coastline, bigger facilities were required to dock, load, maintain, construct, voyage, and trade – the ubiquitous elements of maritime exchange that linked together eventually all parts of the world in stages of what we now call "globalization." Those piers and shipyards were alive with work and financial vitality. This enterprise built institutions, organizations, associations, and personal fortunes, and contributed to every aspect of social and political life whenever and wherever people chose to settle by the sea. Breakwaters and cargo handling technology, financial exchanges, banks and trading companies, manufacturing firms, unions, connecting roads and canals, trains, city architecture, churches and cemeteries, civic and social institutions—all these functions and their physical and economic consequences were a direct, progressive reflection of the energy and accomplishment of the working coast. Indeed, the world was parsed and defined by energy generated by the connective power of the ocean.

History brought scale, further exploration, science and invention, confrontation, and imperial expansion to the world, enabled as a response to the value perceived and desired. Expeditions opened the last places; technology enabled us to explore beneath the surface of the sea; iron, steel, and steam transformed ships in size, speed range, and power. Work, work, work – every aspect of this growth of centuries was powered by the human mind and hand, applied to the opportunities offered by the sea and serviced from the land. One can look at the entirety of world history and reduce it to one word: maritime – defined as "living or found in or near the ocean."

That connection is not purely geographical; rather, it is the unity of effort that is the nature of work and that, when applied well to purpose, can build a world for the benefit of all mankind. This work is applicable and necessary to the future, even as work changes and technology creates new vocations. Today, many people are migrating from inland to coast; coasts are challenged by sea level rise and extreme weather; ports can become teleports and cyber-ports seemingly indifferent to traditional structures. But here is a fact not well known: almost all data, financial transactions, internet informational transfers, communications, and more, move at light-speed through cables deep on the ocean floor where, invisible, they connect us coast to coast, underwater.

THE LEISURE EDGE

The edge where land and sea intersect is also a place for leisure. We go there for a walk, whether solitary or romantic, the gathering of family, a place for children to play and remember, a rendezvous of friends where we eat and drink and sing songs before an open fire, waves crashing just beyond our line of sight, where we can relax in freedom from our worldly concerns.

The beach has been portrayed culturally in art and literature with timeless seascapes of curving sand, enveloping dunes, waves benign, and men and women in bathing suits. The primary and secondary dunes that typically separate the beach from inland act as protective curtains of privacy, natural grassy barriers that buffer beachgoers from their quotidian concerns and a return to work. Long stairs descend, the sting of sand is felt, the smell and sound of the ocean displaces cares and concerns left behind, even for an afternoon.

While beaches were at one time a place for work – harvesting fish and shellfish – they have now become a space for leisure, even when they pass before some mighty row of private residences, condominiums, and hotels that have encroached forward to diminish the border of the regenerative sea.

There is erosion there – not just the inundation by storm waves to undermine the foundations of those intrusive structures – but also by the dissolution of other protections, which have always sheltered land from sea. Beaches are privatized; resorts and clubs claim exclusive lengths of the endless sand; entertainment piers are built as artificial land onto which the culture of rides and cotton candy extends. Solitude is shattered by the compulsively active gas-powered vehicles, small boats and kayaks to rent, surf and paddle boards, wind surfers and sail kites, vendors, even hustlers and beggars who prey on the distraction of fun. Suddenly, there is jaunty music everywhere, peace and quiet gone, even the crashing surf masked by amplified artificial pitch and beat. The shells and driftwood are collected and burnt; the birds fed hotdogs and popcorn, their nesting grounds trampled; the sand and beach grasses clogged with plastic detritus, broken glass, and garbage. What has happened? The openness and tranquility and value of the edge is gone.

We have arrived, invaded, overwhelmed with all our numbers: our umbrellas and wind screens, barbecues and beach chairs, boisterous games, mechanical devices, territorial expectations, and innumerable crass instruments of distraction and commercial consumption. There is a television ad depicting a father loaded down with all this stuff like a 21st-century beast of burden, trudging to his four-wheel drive SUV parked, not in a land-side designated lot, but down on the beach, on the surf line itself, another aggressive symbol of status in which to drive his family home, leaving multiple tire tracks to scar the once pristine sand as if it were just another indifferent highway.

This seems all wrong to me. I say the beaches belong to everyone, the coast around. Every beach is a reserve, a protected area for natural systems, marine creatures, sea birds, coastal flora and fauna *and* people – yes, all the people who will use it sustainably, leave their destructive habits and unrecyclable junk on land already despoiled, and value the edge for all its natural capacity for recreation, renewal, and regeneration. California and some other states have declared the coast from top to bottom a public amenity. Some cities have done so, building public access and pathways the whole way around in place of exclusive commerce and industrialization better placed elsewhere.

I say free the ocean edge, give it back in pure form so we can all enjoy the plentitude it gives to us. Let the kids play and swim without equipment; let them search the tid pools for the critters that live there; let them feel things, like wet and hot, dry and cold. Let them come to the edge in all seasons so they can experience change, feel anger and solace in the sound of the sea, be by themselves if they want to be, and be together in a place where they can connect authentically, to each other, siblings, parents, even strangers, in a community of pure value, natural structure, and rewarding behavior.

THE SECURITY EDGE

We are discussing the edge, where the land meets the sea – the hard edge, soft edge, working edge, leisure edge – various perspectives brought to bear on this most dynamic place. But what about the security edge? What does the specific configuration of the coast provide to protect us from natural and human intrusions?

The most obvious answer is the barrier: the curvature, inclination, geology, and natural configuration provided. The very shape of the land protects us from strong wind and angry wave. The points of land and sheltered coves, the beach and barrier dunes, the mangrove swamps, the rocky cliffs and bluffs – all these contribute to the security of human settlements there. In many cases, we have exploited those features to site our cities and settlements. We have, for example, extended protections by adding breakwaters and engineered port facilities or designated certain beaches as resorts and recreational opportunity.

We have also destroyed many of those features – blasted artificial ports, removed and filled the mangroves, dredged the natural river outlets, and created coastal features and constructions that modify and erode rather than sustain the coastal zone. As extreme weather events increase and as the sea level rises, these man-made artificial features are challenged and proven short-sighted with serious social and economic disruption.

Another important aspect of the security edge is defense against military attack. Historically, ports became targets; beaches were likely places for attack; bluffs and out-crops provided sites for observation and artillery; coastal features were logical places for bunkers, look-out towers, radar placements, and other structures for defense. One can see the ruins of these installations – old forts overlooking coastal cities with rusting cannon as physical memorials to transformational battles and events. The narrow entrances to the Baltic Sea at Oresund and Mediterranean Sea at Gibraltar are such important historical places, where access was limited, tolls collected, and passage surveyed, even prohibited as an expression of political and economic power and potential.

It is no different today. The coast is still the only place for naval construction, bases and fleet stations, submarine pens, missile launch sites, and global communications towers and links to orbiting satellites. Key topographical places are often in the news, passages through which concentrated shipping must pass; a global network of narrow ocean places where movement is confined between two coasts and vulnerable to military surveillance and attack.

We must remember that for all time the ocean has been vast stage for naval operation, imperial expansion, offensive and defensive conflict, and the exercise of national interest. Almost all developed nations have some level of a naval fleet to patrol and police their territorial water against smuggling, piracy, and illegal fishing practice. The larger geopolitical players – the United States and Russian Federation, for example – have massive investments in surface and submarine vessels that are constantly at sea as part as a tactical game of influence. Growing economies like China and India are engaged in a costly expansion of technology and capacity to compete on the world ocean for strategic advantage; another version of the arms race with implications for future control of the sea.

All this may seem invisible and disconnected from how we understand and view the edge. But it is real and significant; security is very much part of what is a multi-layered interpretation of what it means to live alongshore where the land meets the sea, a sharp edge that is both useful and dangerous.

REVEALING THE OCEAN FLOOR

Where am I? A fundamental question – personally existential, institutionally relevant to measure, define, and assert a position in time and space. We have tools to help: the compass, the map, the geo-location device, translating the unknown to the known and indicating a way forward.

At first, it was the wilderness, terrestrial density that needed exploration and conquest by which to build our cities, our factories, our economies, our nation-states. Technology helped; invention as wayfinding tools to survey new ground, set courses, draw boundaries, establish limits to protect territorial claims, lines not to cross without passport or permission, lines to cross in case of conflict or territorial aspiration. We are here: at this latitude and longitude, along this highway, at this moment, accurately, justifiable, and indisputable.

And then it was space – a vast new dimension that, by scale alone, demanded even more extensive, sophisticated technology – more physics, astronomical calculation, exploratory vehicles, satellite observations, software, amplifying our capacity to measure the earth below and space beyond to a decimal of almost infinite precision. What was left?

Oh yes, the ocean – that, while representing only 0.05 percent of the Earth's total mass, nonetheless covers 70% of its planetary surface in layers of fluid mystery, a place of danger and darkness, subject to literary fantasy and occasional daring exploit and invention – yes, charted and mapped, but to always surprising inadequacy and incompleteness. "We know more about the surface of Mars than we do the ocean," is the oft-quoted statement of condition.

In the fall of 2019, a partnership was announced between The Nippon Foundation, a Japanese philanthropy with demonstrated ocean interest, and the International Hydrographic Organization to undertake SEABED 2030, a collaborative project that aims to bring together all available data to produce A General Bathymetric Chart of the Ocean by that year, complete and open to the public. The project is seen as a major contribution to the United Nations Sustainable Development Goal 14: "to conserve and sustainably use the oceans, seas, and marine resources for sustainable development."

The purpose is to understand the relationship between the ocean floor and circulation, climate and weather patterns, tides, wave action and energy conversion, sediment transport, tsunami wave propagation, underwater geo-hazards, and other physical phenomena and obstacles to the utility of the world ocean; to include, one presumes, everything from fisheries to underwater cables, from deep sea mining to offshore oil/gas exploration, from data collection to applied technology and invention, all of which to be consolidated into a central repository (ironically located in Boulder, Colorado), and made available to all interests.

The data will be collected by multi-beam echosounder equipment housed aboard such platforms as public and private research vessels, commercial ships in transit, fishing boats, and autonomous underwater ROVers, specifically to investigate the 93% of the ocean floor below 200 meters (the shallower inshore territorial waters to be charted by national agencies), through the participation of some 40 international organizations and networks across more than 50 countries, to include such distinguished institutions as the Alfred Wegener Institute (Germany), National Institute of Water and Atmospheric Research (New Zealand), Lamont Doherty Earth Observatory (United States), Stockholm University (Sweden), University of

New Hampshire Center for Coastal and Ocean Mapping (United States), and the British Oceanographic Data Centre (United Kingdom). The project is complicated, ambitious, and expensive.

The cost is estimated at some US$3 billion. To put that into perspective, the cumulative cost, adjusted for inflation, just for the US National Atmospheric and Space Agency (NASA) space program is estimated at US$1.17 trillion. How much of the value inherent in the knowledge deriving from space exploration has actually benefited the world economy? The sponsors of SEABED 2030 assert that this mapping project is vital "to the security, safety, and economic health of a 'blue economy' estimated at US$1.5 trillion per year and some 31 million full-time jobs worldwide.

So, where are we? The Nippon Foundation envisions a path forward, with clarity of purpose and action, with new technical tools and institutional cooperation, and with generous stimulus funding to unfold the ocean's layers of fluid mystery, to enlighten a last place of danger and darkness, of wilderness now measured, unlimited, and known.

What's left? The human psyche awaits.

THE FLATTENED OCEAN

Ancient people believed the earth was flat. We presume to know better now; indeed, the term "flat-earther" is used today as a derogatory comment for those who hold such antiquated views. But when you consider how we depict our world as land and sea we use still two dimensions, length and breadth, in the form of maps and charts – and even the frame of our modern navigation devices and computer screens. Only recently, have we been able to manipulate knowledge as recorded data in a volumetric third dimension that can be visualized as historically documented change and projected possibility for the future. This is a radically new way to view the world.

I was fascinated by a presentation by Dr. Whitney Barlow Robles from Harvard University at a conference on Water History, titled *Flattening Sea Life in the 18th*

Century. While this was a narrow iteration of the flattened ocean, it contained obvious and not-so-obvious observations regarding the collection, transmission, and accumulation of knowledge into what we call "science," and how it is applied to a socio-political dynamic.

Natural scientists – our first explorers – joined ship passages and organized expeditions to observe the miracles of a world expanding through transportation, trade, and dominion. They collected specimens on lengthy passages, painted images, described characteristics, and pressed samples onto paper in two dimensions as their contributions to writing "the book of Nature." Such compendia were easily transported aboard ship and stored in personal and institutional libraries. Our early scientific societies became the lively outlet for sharing this knowledge, and the curiosities assembled became the core of major museums whose collections rely heavily on that effort to this day. The journals, sketch books, diagrams, and crude charts became tools for visualizing the world in books, maps, projections, sailing instructions, and even visualization as flattened "skins" on the surfaces of globes: large ones in the halls of science, and pocket ones in the kit of scientists and explorers of ensuing generations. The exchange of such documents was an historical form of "paperwork" exchanged among peers as in The Enlightenment, we accumulated what might be called "Atlantic" or western science, based on an apparently inexhaustible supply of new information.

Dr. Robles suggested some interesting further ideas derived from this history. In some cases, the species and data assembled was collected by slaves; the exchange of such information became a text in the sharing of concepts and cultural values; awareness of astronomy, anthropology, gastronomy, economics, and historical process was enhanced though these artifacts; and the exchange of such "documents" enabled imperial extension, governance, and communication to amplify in parallel with the physical exchange of goods, people, and ideas. The ocean was the conduit for all this as the surface of connection. When that surface was in tumult, ships, men, cargo, and knowledge were lost.

The connections to circumstance today are obvious. When we find lost ships, we approach them as new-found knowledge that will confirm, modify or deny what we think we know from the past. When we explore the ocean, we collect ever more data, documenting a still astonishingly unknown part of the world with underwater and satellite observation in minute and comprehensive detail. And that, too, miniaturized, is expressed in two dimensions in our academic papers, graphs and presentations, data visualizations and calculation models, and real-time videos and documentary films through which we parse what we know about the world. Even our reports, plans, regulations, legislative proposals, laws, treaties, and secrets are communicated in this flattened form. Despite all our progress, we still express and understand in only two dimensions.

How do we add dimensionality to our thinking? When you look at the sky, how many dimensions do you see? The same question can be applied to the ocean, where we see only a composition of water and atmosphere divided by the horizon line. But the ocean, most decidedly, is not flat. It is a multi-dimensional place of change and exchange that encompasses, and relates to, every aspect of our being. We will never truly understand it seeing only length and breadth; we must find depth, not just in the form of soundings – so many feet surface to bottom, here or there – but, most importantly, in the form of integrated response in every aspect, every dimension, of our future. The ocean is as deep and wide as history and as essential as knowledge itself.

MANGROVES
Visitors to islands and coastal areas just north and south of the equator are familiar with the dense growth of mangrove trees native to those regions. We probably don't give mangroves much thought, but, like everything in Nature, they serve an extraordinary range of beneficial uses.

For example, they are the basis of a complex marine food chain that begins as their leaves drop into tidal waters and are colonized by marine bacteria that convert carbon compounds into a nitrogen rich detritus that, covered with microorganisms, becomes food for the smallest animals such as worms, snails, shrimp, mollusks and other shellfish, and for larger fish, many of which are harvested by man, some of which are now endangered.

In addition, mangrove forests provide shelter and breeding habitat, filter and assimilate pollutants from up-land run-off, stabilize bottom sediments, improve water quality, and provide important protection against shoreline erosion. There is no question that mangrove zones are important barriers against storm surge and extreme wave action, including tsunamis.

The total worldwide mangrove area is estimated at not less than 170,000 square kilometers and includes some sixty endemic species of trees and shrubs. But as with so many other elements in the coastal zone, mangrove forests are under extreme pressure as a result of toxic poison from wastes, both human and industrial, and the increasing value – hence increasing demand – for new coastal land reclaimed for shrimp farming and other aquaculture, waste disposal, industry, and residential and leisure development. Some research indicates that more than 50% of the world's mangrove forests have succumbed to such pressures in the past 25 years.

Does anybody care? The International Society for Mangrove Ecosystems is a global mangrove constituency that has adopted a charter for coastal protection that complements the World Charter for Nature, proclaimed by the United Nations in 1982, affirming that Nature shall be respected, genetic viability on earth shall not be compromised, conservation shall be practiced, sustainable management shall be utilized by man, and Nature shall be secured against degradation. The reader has surely noticed that, in the interval since this proclamation, destruction of mangrove environments, and much else, has continued unabated.

Nonetheless, there is an effort to protect and reclaim mangrove forests in Florida, the Caribbean, and elsewhere. An interesting experiment is taking place in Eritrea where an effort is underway to restore mangrove trees in traditional areas as a source of foliage fodder for goats and sheep, as well as for seed that can be dried into a grain-like food staple for humans. The planting, tending, harvesting and use of these by-products are seen as a strategy to relieve the terrible poverty in that land.

The experiment has extended into the desert. Young trees – lightly fertilized, irrigated with salt water, and well-drained to protect from the over-concentration of salt – have flourished, allowing scientists to envision a new forest covering large areas previously deemed infertile contributors to CO_2 conversion and climate change. The experiment reduces irrigation demand on the limited local fresh water supply, and provides a new avenue for labor and community betterment.

In the ocean environment, no single element can be disconnected from the next. A mangrove tree may seem irrelevant, but it is the cornerstone of a vital nutrient system for marine organisms, a structure that naturally protects and cleanses coastal areas, and an important contributor to human health and well-being.

CORAL REEFS

Coral reefs are often referred to as the rainforests of the sea. Given their immense biodiversity, confined to relatively little space, perhaps the reference should really be the other way around: rainforests are the coral reefs of the land!

At the level of phyla – the broadest taxonomic organization in the kingdom of animals (the major groupings of animals, plants, fungi and protists are called kingdoms) – coral reefs harbor 33 of the 38 known animal phyla – more than any other ecosystem on the planet. By contrast, tropical rainforests host only 8 phyla. Some rainforests may have more species, but coral reefs harbor a greater overall diversity of life. Estimates range from 100,000 to greater than one million species living on coral reefs.

Much has been written on the beauty, color and splendor of coral reefs. They evoke a range of images and associations: from clear blue waters and lazy days under the sun, to excitement in exploring the unknown – unfamiliar animals and life forms, thoughts of adventure, shipwrecks and sunken treasure. Perhaps more importantly, they provide resources for millions of coastal people worldwide – the only readily available source of protein, and crucial livelihoods. Corals and related animals also provide a cornucopia of pharmaceutical compounds, with new cancer treatments and wonder drugs being discovered regularly.

But, unfortunately, the plight of coral reefs is now equally well known. Over the course of one human generation, most coral reefs have declined around the world.

The causes include a range of insults occurring as a consequence of our ever-expanding population, especially along our coastal zones. For example, of the 17 mega-cities around the world (i.e. those cities containing more than 10 million people), 14 occur within the coastal zone. Not all of these cities are adjacent to coral reefs, but most between the tropics of Cancer and Capricorn are – especially in Asia – and they rely upon the ecosystem services of coral reefs to some important degree, whether for products, shoreline protection or tourism revenue. The Millennium Ecosystem Assessment found that within the coastal zone, the vast majority of people live in close proximity to reefs.

We are adding population to coastal lands, and many of these people are consuming more than our ecosystems can produce, and mismanaging their by-products and wastes. Threats of over-fishing, excessive sedimentation from deforestation and coastal land transformation, untreated sewage, unregulated agriculture and other forms of mismanagement all stress coral reefs and associated ecosystems such as mangrove and sea grass habitats.

It is also increasingly apparent that impacts from climate change – in the form of higher sea surface temperatures, increased erosion from changed ocean chemistry, more powerful storms, and sea level rise – will bring repeated shocks to coral reefs in the coming years and decades ahead. The outlook for reefs is not good, unless we can halt the degradation, and quickly. A recently published paper in the journal *Science* suggests that levels of CO_2 could become unsustainable for coral within 50 years, dooming reefs worldwide.

Corals are invertebrate animals belonging to the phylum cnidaria (along with the jellyfishes and sea anemones), with stinging cells (cnidocytes), as a distinguishing characteristic. A coral's basic body structure is simple: a vase-like sac (known as a polyp) with a hole in one end (the mouth), surrounded by stinging tentacles that capture food. To feed, a coral polyp will extend its tentacles out from its body and wave them in the water current, where they encounter small plankton or other food particles, and capture prey with their tentacles' stinging cells.

Coral polyps extract abundant calcium from surrounding seawater, which they use to create a hardened structure for protection and growth. Coral reefs are created by millions of tiny polyps forming large carbonate structures, and are the basis of a framework and home for hundreds of thousands, if not millions, of other species. Coral reefs form the largest biological structures on earth; they are only ones distinctly visible from space.

The coral reefs evolved over the past 200- to 300-million years. Over this history, corals have developed an advanced form of symbiosis, or a mutually-beneficial living arrangement, with tiny single-celled plants known as *zooxanthellae*. Inside the tissues of each coral polyp live these microscopic, single-celled algae. These two groups – animal and plant – share space, gas exchange and nutrients to survive.

Therefore, while corals are animals, they function like plants in many respects, explaining why reef-building corals are confined to living so near the surface of the water where they are easily reached by sunlight. The symbiosis between plant and animal also underlies the colors of corals, so appealing to divers on a reef. Vital sunlight drives corals to compete for space on the sea floor, constantly pushing the limits of their physiological tolerances in a competitive environment among so many different species. However, it also makes corals highly susceptible to environmental stress.

Many coral species reproduce once or twice each year. Most spawn by releasing eggs and sperm into the water, but the period of spawning varies from one species to another. Other coral species, with limited distribution, are brooders. This baby coral looks like a tiny jellyfish and floats around near the surface, before descending in the water column until it finds a suitable space to call home – usually a hard surface to which it can attach.

In general, massive corals tend to grow slowly, increasing in size from 0.5 cm to 2 cm per year. However, under favorable conditions, some species can grow as much as 4.5 cm per year. In contrast to the massive species, branching colonies tend to grow much faster. Under favorable conditions, these colonies can grow vertically by as much as 10 cm per year.

Based on current estimates, shallow water coral reefs occupy somewhere between 284,000 and 512,000 km2 of the planet. If all the world's shallow water coral reefs were crammed together, it would take up an area roughly equivalent to the size of Ecuador. This area represents less than 0.015 percent of the ocean, yet coral reefs harbor more than one quarter of the ocean's biodiversity – an amazing ratio. No other global ecosystem occupies such a limited area with so many life forms. Coral reefs are found in both tropical and subtropical waters, in a zone extending from 30°N to 30°S of the equator. Reef-building corals do not grow at depths of over 30 m (100 ft) or where the water temperature falls below 16 °C (72 °F).

Charles Darwin originally classified coral reefs by their structure and morphology, describing them as: 1) "fringing reefs, fairly narrow and recently formed, that lie near emergent land, separated from the coast by a navigable channel, sometimes incorrectly termed a 'lagoon';" 2) "barrier reefs, broader and separated from the coast by a stretch of water up to several miles wide and several tens of meters deep"; 3) "sandy islands, covered with a characteristic pattern of vegetation that have sometimes formed on top of a barrier reef, the coastline broken by passes, which have occupied the beds of former rivers; and atolls, large, ring-shaped reefs lying off the coast, with a lagoon in their middle, the emergent part of the reef often covered with accumulated sediments and characteristic vegetation consisting primarily of coconut trees."

Coral reefs support an extraordinary biodiversity. They are home to a variety of tropical fishes, such as the colorful parrot fish, angelfish, damselfish and butterfly fish. Other fish found on coral reefs include groupers, snappers, grunts and wrasses, amounting to over 4,000 species in all. Reefs provide spawning ground, nursery, refuge and feeding areas to myriad other organisms: sponges, sea anemones, worms, crustaceans (including shrimp, spiny lobsters and crabs), mollusks (including cephalopods), echinoderms (including starfish, sea urchins and sea cucumbers), sea squirts, sea turtles and sea snakes. Reefs also play an important role as natural breakwaters, which minimize the wave impacts from storms such as cyclones, hurricanes or typhoons. Some reports indicate, for example, that the extent of damage caused by the Asian Tsunami in 2004 was far less in areas in close proximity to healthy reefs areas than those close to degraded ones.

The stunning beauty of coral reefs makes them a powerful magnet for tourists, and well–managed tourism provides a sustainable means of earning foreign currency and employment for people around the world, even in remote areas of developing countries.

Several attempts have been made to estimate the values of coral reefs in terms of dollars. Benefits from coral reefs can be categorized into two types: "direct use values" (fisheries and tourism industries, for instance), and "indirect use values" (benefits from coastline protection, for example). According to a United Nations estimate, the total economic value of coral reefs ranges from US$100,000 to 600,000 per square kilometer per year.

Coral bleaching occurs when the symbiosis between corals and their symbiotic zooxanthellae breaks down. This results in the loss of the brown symbionts and a rapid whitening or bleaching of the coral host. This is a stress response by the coral host. If the temperature decreases temporarily, the stressed coral can recover; if it persists, the affected colony can die.

The impacts from coral bleaching are becoming global, and are increasing in frequency and intensity. Mass coral bleaching generally happens when temperatures around coral reefs exceed 1C above the area's historical norm for 4 or more weeks. Sea surface temperature increases have been strongly associated with El Niño weather patterns. However, light intensity during flat calm conditions also plays a critical role in triggering bleaching response. If temperatures climb to more than 20C for similar or longer periods, coral mortality following bleaching increases.

Mass coral bleaching was not documented in the scientific literature before 1979; however, significant mass bleaching events were reported in 1982, 1987, and 1992. The strongest sea surface warming event ever recorded occurred in 1998, in which an estimated 46% of corals in the western Indian Ocean were heavily impacted or died. In 2005, sea surface temperatures in the Caribbean were the highest reported in more than 100 years. These reports continue.

Extensive and poorly managed land development also threaten coral reefs. Within the last 20 years, once-prolific mangrove forests are being destroyed. Nutrient-rich water causes fleshy algae and phytoplankton to thrive in coastal areas in suffocating amounts known as algal blooms that disrupt the nutrient balance of reef communities. Thus, the losses of wetlands and mangrove habitats are significant factors affecting water quality on inshore reefs, in turn causing the spread of infectious diseases among corals.

And, as if this were not enough, coral reefs are suffering from the paradoxical situation that we are loving them to death. Visitors to reefs add stress, in some cases tipping the balance such that immune-suppressed corals become susceptible to further disease spread, and, more often than not, die. In addition, the marine souvenir and curio trade is responsible for denuding of reefs all around the world – corals are taken for jewelry and as live rock for aquariums, and reef fishes and other organisms are sold in preserved form in trinket shops and alive in pet shops. According to the U.S. Coral Reef Action Plan, the U.S. is the world's largest importer of ornamental coral reef species, and as such has a critical responsibility to address degradation of coral reef ecosystems that may arise from destructive collection practices and unsustainable trade. The U.S. has banned the use of most destructive fishing practices, and collection of stony corals and live rock are prohibited in most federal, state and territorial waters. However, unenlightened tourists from around the world continue to join their American counterparts to buy reef souvenirs, unwittingly contributing to the dramatic decline of reefs globally.

In order to protect coral reefs and other marine environments effectively, it is imperative to manage our uses and impacts so that they do not exceed the self-repair capacity. The biological and physical processes influencing coral reefs are generally much larger than the management ability of governments and communities. However, most of the human actions that damage coral reefs can be managed locally. A variety of activities, including education, establishment of international conventions and treaties, research projects, and the establishment of marine protected areas are under way to protect coral reefs.

One of the most important things that can be done is to spread awareness about the value and services that coral reefs (and their related ecosystems, such as mangroves and sea grasses) provide, and to encourage communities, companies and governments to take steps to protect them. The International Coral Reef Initiative (ICRI), designated 2008 as the International Year of the Reef, and organized a year-long campaign of events and initiatives hosted by governments, individuals, corporations, and schools around the world to communicate the serious challenge posed to reef systems, to build awareness and understanding of reef value and services, and to strengthen near-term action and long-term support for coral reef conservation.

Since 1994, the ICRI, has served as an informal partnership of governments, international organizations, Non-Governmental Organizations and scientists. It was established out of concern about the degradation of coral reefs. The Initiative is one of fourteen multilateral environmental agreements, programs, partnerships and networks relevant to the protection and conservation of coral reefs. In addition, many Non-Governmental Organizations have included coral reef protection within the priorities of their marine programs, including the World Wildlife Fund, the Nature Conservancy, Conservation International, the Global Coral Reef Monitoring Network, Reef Base, the Coral Reef Alliance, the Reef Check Foundation, the Coral Reef Initiative for the South Pacific, and the Meso-American Barrier Reef System Project.

The global situation regarding these diverse and valuable marine ecosystems is dire, but hope is not lost. Through such efforts as the International Year of the Reef, we can expect greater support for conservation and greater political will to tackle the many stressors that coral reefs face. Let's hope it's not too late to stem the tide of reef degradation, for the world will be a significantly poorer place if coral reefs continue to disappear from our oceans.

SARGASSO SEA

I am often asked how it is possible to understand, much less advocate for, something as vast and complicated as the ocean. My thought has been to document and describe for the public every aspect of the ocean, a task that is outright impossible by virtue of my limited time and understanding. One tactic is to release the power of metaphor, to find one feature that is both symbol and reality of all the rest. There is such a place; it is called the Sargasso Sea.

The area, located in the Atlantic Ocean, off Bermuda, is specifically defined, not by land, but by surrounding sea: four ocean currents – North Atlantic to the north, Gulf Stream to the west, Equatorial to the south, and Canary to the east – dynamic flows that circumscribe "the space" as a gyre, turning clockwise, deep and clear and ecologically unique. It is a natural intersection, as if the epicenter of all oceanic systems, rich in biology, marine wildlife, and Sargassum, accumulation of 'golden' algae in floating rafts, on, in, and under which ocean life teems with vitality. It is a place for spawning, breeding, nesting, and feeding, for migrating birds and whales, for sharks, sailfish, tuna, marlin, wahoo, and dolphin; for resident, sheltering eels, turtles, mollusks, crustaceans, bacteria and other microscopic creatures. It shelters seamounts, ridges, and coral reefs. It enables temperature, oxygen production and carbon sequestration. It mixes the exchange of value from its underwater sources. It is an encyclopedia of ocean knowledge and exceptional area for research and monitoring of ocean systems. While perhaps not as extensive as other wild places, it is certainly as vital as any natural environment on Earth.

It is also a crossroads for human endeavor: for shipping, fishing, harvesting, polluting, and accumulating the detritus of consumption, primarily as plastic, in all its forms, discarded the world over and brought by ocean circulation to this one fluid, intense concentration of waste much publicized worldwide in the popular press as "the North Atlantic Garbage Patch."

It is also a place for history and myth: the area of the so-called Bermuda Triangle, where ships are strangely becalmed, inexplicably disappeared, where surely sirens and naiads must lurk.

Thus, Sargasso is evocative symbol and distinctive reality of all the forces that characterize the ocean and its interconnections to all aspects of life on Earth, human and otherwise. As such, it is both real and ephemeral, particular and general, nurturing and destroying, embodying both the problems and solutions, questions and answers we seek to study, explain, and conserve. Ironically, while so dramatically affected by human behavior, it exists on the high seas, mostly outside the exclusive economic zone of Bermuda, and thus beyond authority and regulation by any state or government. Some 50% of the ocean area exists in this socio-political limbo; again, Sargasso stands for the challenge to all that unregulated, unprotected area beyond any encompassing framework for national jurisdiction. How, then, do we protect and conserve such a place?

On March 11, 2014 governments came together in Bermuda to sign the Hamilton Declaration on Collaboration for the Conservation of the Sargasso Sea, the result of a two-year negotiation between interested governments that are either located in the broader Sargasso Sea area or have an interest in high seas conservation. The Hamilton Declaration was initially signed by the Azores, Bermuda, Monaco, UK and US, who were later joined by the British Virgin Islands, the Bahamas, Canada, the Cayman Islands, and most recently the Dominican Republic.

The Sargasso Sea Commission was thereafter formed to: 1) promote international recognition of the unique ecological and biological nature and global significance of the Sargasso Sea; (2) encourage scientific research to expand existing knowledge of the Sargasso Sea ecosystem in order to further assess its health, productivity and resilience; and (3) develop proposals for submission to existing regional, sectoral and international organizations to promote the objectives of the Hamilton Declaration.

Various sectoral organizations that have joined this effort include: The International Commission for the Conservation of Atlantic Tuna (fisheries), the United Nations International Maritime Organization (shipping), and the International Seabed Authority (mining), plus other non-governmental organizations and academic institutions, creating a network of protection measures toward the establishment of an International Marine Protected Area. It is a determined work in progress.

Reality? Symbol? Both must endure as a force for our personal commitment to the world ocean.

CONNECTION

For many, the ocean is a place apart, a vast wilderness extending beyond our physical and psychological htorizons about which we know very little, at once alien and indifferent, fascinating and compelling.

Consider these facts:

- The ocean covers 71% of the earth's surface.
- The ocean is a central element in the recycling and purification of fresh water.
- The ocean provides 90% of the world's protein, especially in developing nations.
- 60% of the world's population lives within 100 kilometers of an ocean coast.
- The ocean is essential to human survival as a primary source of food, water, climate, and community – immediate, universal, and undeniable. In short, the ocean is the determinant ecology in which we live – the sea connects all things.

If, indeed, all life is dependent on the ocean, then this understanding calls for its new definition as:

- an inter-connected, global eco-system that integrates natural process, habitat, and species with human intervention and impact;
- a comprehensive social system that integrates human needs and actions;
- and a complex political system that connects all peoples worldwide through economic interests, cultural traditions, and cooperative governance.

When we envision the ocean as a wilderness, we are ignoring the reality of the ocean as a domesticated place where humans have left their mark throughout history by exploration and exploitation, immigration and trade, and the exchange of custom and culture. To look from a satellite, one can see that the ocean is marked constantly by the tracks of ships, the tools of globalization through marine transport as old as the ancient Han in the Pacific, the Phoenicians in the Mediterranean, and the Vikings in the Atlantic.

AQUA / TERRA

What has changed over time, however, is the impact of human population growth. The use of the ocean has increased exponentially so that the ocean evinces a shift from abundance to scarcity and from accommodation to conflict.

This is well exemplified by the crisis in fisheries. Research has documented the collapse of certain species such as cod, which once formed the staple diet of much of North America and Europe. This loss is the result of a complex of causes, including unrestricted catch, the advent of efficient gear and technology, and the unwillingness of fishers, both artisanal and industrial, to work cooperatively toward a sustainable harvest. This problem was compounded by the difficulty of regulation due to lack of jurisdiction outside of national economic zones, the inability to monitor or enforce quotas, and the failure of governance to address the challenge.

There are many other examples. What underlies them all, however, is that just as there are social causes to these problems, there must be social solutions. We can complain and accuse and litigate, much as we do for similar behavior on land, but the true solution lies with our determination to deal with our need to domesticate Nature, terrestrial or marine, for human use and to engage in the dialogue and change required to conserve and sustain all natural resources for the benefit of all mankind.

A MARITIME NATION

Americans have no real understanding of our history as a maritime nation. The subject is mostly absent from the texts, and the specific maritime histories have been, most often, enumerations of customs house documents, ship voyages, and the odd naval battle. Only recently has that begun to change, as historians from other disciplines have discovered the broad impact and richness of maritime endeavor as a core theme in the American narrative.

Let's take two points of view: internal and external. If you look at the topography of our nation, you see a system of watersheds: great lakes connected to rivers and the sea; streams descending from major mountain systems, east and west; and myriad rivers feeding the Mississippi, a central north-south artery that splits the nation. Those waterways were the paths of early exploration and settlement. Many of our largest inland cities are located on the confluence of navigable rivers. The Erie Canal, an engineering marvel, linked the heartland to the east coast ports and Europe. Lewis and Clark followed the rivers and streams into the west, through the Rockies to the Pacific. Along these waterways passed the grain, cotton, tobacco, and other agricultural products, the iron and steel and coal and timber, and the manufactured goods, distributed internally, to the eastern ports like New York, Boston, Charleston, and Savannah and around Cape Horn to western ports of San Francisco and Seattle and beyond, as the essence of an emerging American world trade.

The external perspective is also instructive. It reveals that trade is more than export: rather, the exchange of goods from Europe and further east, and, most importantly, the imported return – the arrival of immigrants, refugees from religious tyranny, entrepreneurs, and outlaws, our fore-bears by the thousands. We honor our remaining indigenous people. The rest of us came from away, from Ireland, Scotland and England, from Scandinavia, from Germany and Italy, from Africa (albeit an involuntary passage), and, eventually, from all the nations of the world, these diverse ethnicities combining to create the complex nation that we are. Most of these people came by ship across oceans, and, today, perhaps by different vessels, they are still coming.

Historian Howard Zinn, author of *The People's History of the United States*, offered a contrarian view of American history that should be read by everyone, regardless of political persuasion. Zinn provides a provocative alternative perspective on our nation's story as institutionalized in the text books, a telling argument for taking a second look from a different point of view at something as complex and dynamic as human history.

What Zinn and other historians have recognized is that the principal value exchanged by this process was not just the trade goods and financial accountings, but also the ideas and beliefs, the art, the music, and the literature that constitute our cultural fabric. We listen to world music and appreciate world art. We are open to multiple religions and spiritual practice. We fuse food traditions, fashion, fads, medical treatments, exercise, sport, and language. We may have new and different portals, but the process began long ago, when the first sailors left shore in search of something beyond their own experience, beyond their limited horizon.

When I look at things now, I wonder where the sailors are. We have become fearful and oppositional and close-minded. We have become complacent within our horizon and hostile to new people and new ideas. We need historians like Howard Zinn, or new leaders to show us the way back to the sea from whence our nation came.

THE EXHAUSTED LAND WE LIVE IN

To understand the crises affecting the world ocean, we must first understand the condition of the land around us. For decades, alarms have been sounded to alert us to the exhaustion of the soil. We have experienced a continuing increase in population, in demand for energy, food and fresh water, and in the pollutants derived from our physical, chemical, and biological responses to those requirements. We have come to expect an annual raise, ever increasing quality of life, and sustained returns on our investments – unrealizable without undisciplined personal credit, under-collateralized debt, and unregulated consumption of natural and human resources. Like any Ponzi scheme, we have borrowed against assets once tangible, now increasingly limited, even ephemeral, and can no longer rationalize, postpone, or deny the consequences.

For me, pollution is excess: too much chocolate, too much alcohol, too much fertilizer, too many chemicals, too much waste, too much unregulated consumption indifferent to the needs of an ever-growing community. Too much division and anger. Too much greed, too much inequity, too much injustice. Most simply put: too much too much.

But what about the ocean? I submit that the ocean begins at the mountain-top, and descends to the alluvial plain; that is, everything that occurs on land – be it development, manufacturing, agriculture, or financial enterprise – descends to the sea. It passes in, on, and above the earth in fluid streams of decision, action, and transaction, behaviors that reveal our system of values, be they economic, personal, social, political, or moral.

Specifically, those behaviors impact the downstream, be it effluents that generate red tides along the beaches, or nitrate run-off that eutrophies and suffocates life on the ocean floor, or emissions that rise and fall into the sea to increase the acidity to modify the food chains and to disrupt the breeding and survival of marine plants and animals upon which the system depends. We like to think of the ocean as a place apart, a maritime wilderness, infinitely self-healing and immune to our polluting excesses, but that is not so. Just as we are familiar with the effects of rampant pollution on land, we now know through observation, research and experience that the ocean is also threatened by exhaustion, myriad organic pollutants, declining species, poisoned wildlife, excavated mangroves, developed wetlands, and dead coral. We know that the glaciers are melting at accelerated rates; we know that extreme weather is damaging our coasts in ways unforeseen by our designers and builders. We know coastal communities continue to grow into urban centers making ever-increasing demands on food, water, and energy supplies. We know that many of those settlements have been devastated by tsunami, hurricane and typhoon, and shoreline inundation that has cost millions of dollars and displaced thousands of environmental refugees with no place to go.

To understand the crises affecting the world ocean, we must accept – not deny – these facts, and use this knowledge to mitigate and adapt to these challenges in the short term. Long-term, the problem is more demanding, and may require very different answers to the difficult questions we face.

STAKEHOLDERS IN NATURE

The word "stakeholder" indicates a certain relationship between business and investment. It was apparently first used in the 18th century, referring to individuals who held money during financial transactions or bets – funds held by an independent party in a kind of escrow until the outcome was known of a transaction or wager. The word has evolved into a clearer definition of ownership: a share in a company doing business that has been capitalized through the sale and distribution of fragments of ownership that can be aggregated into influence over policy and management, bought and sold in markets, and used to reward additional investors or successful executives in lieu of salary. There is a clear shift in relationship in this evolution of meaning, from a neutral party to a participant with expectation of return on investment through interest, dividends, or appreciated value.

The word is ubiquitous in policy discussions, referring to individuals, social groups, or greater collectives with an interest in the need for, or outcome of, a government or community policy that affects individual rights, health, security, and well-being of those governed. It seems more and more amorphous through over-use, a cliché by which any interest whatsoever can be described without undue specificity. We are all "stakeholders" in something that enables or disables our interests, depending on the time, place, and details.

While the term is used consistently by the environmental community, it is viewed with suspicion because of its capitalist connotation and with some confusion by its imprecision in the context of human species or terrestrial interest, which are often in conflict despite efforts to combine them into an amalgam of social interest and Nature. It also seems to imply an overly mechanistic or transactional relationship that precludes more emotional and humanistic value questions, psychological and philosophical considerations as viable inclusion in the discussion.

How do we describe the relationship between human society and Nature? In "The Upshot," one of four seminal essays published in1949 in *Sand County Almanac*, Aldo Leopold refers to "the land ethic" that disconnects the relationship from property and ownership. He describes the interaction as shifting from competition to integration – a kind of natural and social symbiosis in which humanity, as a composite of individuals, is one of interdependent parts that "simply enlarges the boundaries of the community to include soils, water, plants, and animals, or collectively, the land." For our purposes, let's make sure that those boundaries are not delimited by land only, and certainly include the sea.

Leopold suggests a "consciousness" that incorporates human behaviors and natural systems that binds our selves and our souls, our outer and inner lives together with all natural things, and forms a kind of ecological continuum in which all things are connected and inter-related in harmony. It was not a new concept by any means; the idea has been discussed by philosophers and theologians since the Greeks, and lived by indigenous peoples for longer. But Leopold's simple statement provided a foundation on which the discipline of "ecology" emerged to "combine life processes, interactions, and adaptations, the movement of materials and energy through living communities, the successional development of ecosystem, and the abundance and distribution of organisms and biodiversity in the context of the environment." Seventy years ago, it was a galvanizing idea that focused the modern environmental movement.

It is still, but for our compulsion to measure and define and organize things in numbers and words, to calculate value in data or dollars, in policies and laws as a practical application of the perspective that for all the progress in science and research has not settled the matter once and for all. The denial of climate change today is the most relevant example – the overwhelming consensus of scientists countered by oppositional, often irrelevant, statistics and circular arguments that question certainty and subvert any response.

This contradiction is inherent in the use of the word "stakeholders." The parties are confused by the notion of property and ownership, science being used in the war between vested interests exclusively opposed to change, and those looking inclusively to adapt to changing circumstance and invent a future. If there is no sense of shared understanding or participatory engagement in this exchange, it is not a conversation at all. If we are to find our way forward, we will need to change this vocabulary, restore ecological connection as a newly articulated framework for action, and assert creative methods for collaboration, integration, and sustainable regeneration in our partnership with the natural world. There is so much at stake.

WATER, WATER EVERYWHERE

We live in a water world, dependent on rainfall, groundwater circulating over land though streams and rivers, and the aquifers beneath our feet. Water is the most precious commodity on earth, in that its supply is finite and limited in distribution, and it is required to survive in the same amount by every one of us every day, rich or poor, wherever we may be. As of July 2010, access to water and sanitation was recognized by the United Nations General Assembly as a basic human right.

We rely on water as an essential component of health and well-being, though it be under constant threat by over-consumption, toxins and pollutants, and waste from industrial and agricultural production, sewage treatment, fracking, fertilizer run-off, emissions, chemical and other manufacturing, and the many other technologies that we have invented to support a developing world populated by some 7 billion worldwide, a number that is projected to grow by another 2 billion by 2030 – a date not that far away.

We will be able to feed this new world, not to mention the millions today who already go hungry, if we increase agricultural yields significantly and sustainably. Globally, rain-fed agriculture is practiced on 80% of cultivated land, which supplies more than 60% of the world's food. According to Aquastat, the United Nations Food and Agricultural Organization (FAO) comprehensive website documenting water demand and use by country, "with so much of the Earth's water being used for agriculture, it's clear that an improvement of water management becomes key…"

Reliance on more efficient irrigation and more sophisticated water management becomes more than imperative once we consider climate change, increasing incidence and intensity of drought, extreme weather, depleted local water sources, corrupted water systems, and other factors contributing to soil infertility and erosion.

FAO cites a stunning example of the consequences of irresponsible irrigation practice in the Aral Sea, when water was withdrawn to irrigate cotton, reducing the annual flow by almost 85%. It was an environmental tragedy. As a result, to paraphrase the FAO Report, sea level fell by 16 meters between 1981 and 1990; 24 species of fish disappeared; local catch, which once totaled over 44,000 tons per year and supported 60,000 jobs, vanished; toxic dust salt from the sea bed made the remaining water hazardous to drink; thousands left the area as environmental refugees while those who remained lost their livelihood. The Aral Sea is just one dramatic example of how water management transcends local practice and demands regional, national, and international planning and management of this declining resource if it is to be conserved for use. If there is a single issue for the international community to agree on as an incontrovertible requirement for world peace, it may be this one: equitable and sustainable water practice and distribution, regardless of other necessities. Given the already extant examples of water conflict, such agreement may be long in coming, if at all.

As with so many things, the solution may not come from such a grand design, but from small, incremental, local actions that will collectively make a difference. For example, farmers who switch from surface flooding to localized irrigation can cut their water use by 30 to 60% and increase yields of most crops by 100 to 400%. I once watched a Chinese farmer transfer a precise number of buckets from a rainwater catchment area onto a field laid out slightly downhill and furrowed and barriered to distribute the water along efficient pathways to individual plants so that when the last bucket was poured at the top the last plant was fully watered below. It was effective, efficient, elegant, and wise.

When the population has grown beyond the projections, we will turn to the ocean for desalinized water, in spite of even the most enlightened methods of water conservation and use. There is a critical window of time: we must not hesitate lest we find ourselves faced with the quandary of water, water everywhere, and not a drop to drink.

FARMERS AND FISHERS

During a visit to the National Maritime Museum in Oslo, Norway, in the Small Boat Hall, I came across a series of diagrams – circles in an almost mandala form that visualized the cycles of the year, of the harvest on both land and at sea, of the work patterns of men and women, and of the inter-relationship of the generations – grandparents, parents, and children – to the sustainability of their remote oceanside communities.

These diagrams were an intellectual and emotional revelation for me, very much a city boy from America's heartland. They provided extraordinary insight into the patterns and practical collaborations among the inhabitants of coastal communities. For the first time, I appreciated the primarily social organization of such enterprise, the inherent wisdom of experience that determined success in a challenging place that demanded the participation of every resident, old and young, in a series of inter-related activities that enabled a healthy, happy, and sustainable livelihood.

Of course, much of this wisdom was based on the observation of the seasons, the changing of the light, temperature, and resultant practicality for growing things ashore. Each season provided its work-list; tasks were assigned to the most able and skilled to perform just those things. The men turned and tilled the land, the women planted, every one harvested. Additional tasks that transformed this bounty into food in the seasons to come included gathering, processing, storing, and even, as seeds, preparing for the repetition of the cycle.

There was also a division of labor related to the sea: gear and boats to be prepared, the fishing itself by crews of men and boys, and the transformation of that harvest into dried fish, export product for trade, and other needs for community life: 100% of the fish was used; for needles, buttons, thread, health products, and skin for clothing and other uses.

There was a further circle – of the social and religious celebrations and events associated with each activity and each season. The sum of the circles was a telling portrait of how society can be organized around the plenty that Nature so generously provides for our well-being.

I received an announcement of a new partnership of the National Family Farm Coalition and the Northwest Atlantic Marine Alliance, wherein the synergy of activity, needs, and political interests between the two was recognized as common threats facing "land food" and "sea food." The partnership affirmed the similar challenges faced by many family farmers and fishers in recent decades: corporate consolidation of food systems at the expense of small- and mid-scale producers, the decline of rural communities, the reduction of food workers, the destruction of environment, the delimited access to real food, and collective health. "The expansion of a more sustainable food future is dependent on this declaration of interdependence and solidarity between us," the release declared, "a vision to unite family farmers, ranchers, and fishers in a collective effort for economic empowerment and food justice."

At issue here is the recurring impact of scale – the growth of food production, from artisanal and local, to industrial and global. That enormous growth has had astonishing impact on national economies, building an international market for certain foods and grains at the expense of other production, of the land saturated with pesticide and nitrate-based fertilizer, of exhausted and poisoned earth blown and eroded away into our streams where it descends through watersheds to the coast, where it subsumes oxygen and biotic life, turning large areas of coastal water into a place where no animal, no plant, and ultimately – deprived of associated livelihood – no human can survive.

Perhaps such destruction, aggravated by climate change and extreme weather, can be overcome by the diminution of scale – the return to the local, to cooperation among those who live by this small-scale production, to the revitalization of land and community by return to sustainable values.

Where I live, there is a strong revival of fishing and agriculture. Our fastest-growing profession is organic farming – young people returned from the city, educated and prepared to pursue hard work as a reflection of quality of life, outdoor living not compromised by the demands of consumption, and fueled by the natural energy of earth and ocean. They are becoming much more politically involved, engaging in the determination of policy and direction, and joining together in value-added enterprise, fairs and markets to which so many of us outliers flock for good food, real value, and investment in the health of all aspects of our community.

So, fishers and farmers, unite! Let those circles and cycles of health and vitality return, revitalized, from an exhibit on the museum wall to a regenerative way by which we can live.

GATHERING IN

My neighbor, Rob McCall, is the author of *Awanadjo Almanac*, a monthly column and podcast on the connection between observation and experience of Nature with our inner selves. He is a quiet master of the form, practiced by other modern writers such as Thoreau and Emerson, as well as more contemporary work by Aldo Leopold, Rachael Carson, Annie Dillard, Noel Perrin, Wallace Stegner, and Terry Tempest Williams. The personal essay is an increasingly popular literary form, caught between poetry and longer prose, using the power of metaphor to provide a sudden realization, framing some juxtaposition or symbiosis as accessible, revelatory insight.

In a recent essay, Rob described the phenomenon of autumnal "gathering in," the collection of the last of the harvest, the late planted vegetables, the seeds to over-winter for the spring, the substance that fills root cellars and canning jars to sustain us through the dark of winter. The animals do the same, of course, collecting and storing what they need in hidden places and dens to which they retreat from the ice, the cold, and the snow.

It was a lovely thought, and it made me wonder about what would be the corresponding seasonal change in the maritime world, what invisible shifts and sustaining commutations might occur alongshore or below the surface of the ocean?

As the sun moves north and the dark descends, surface water becomes colder, declining downwards, colder still, to change patterns of growth and distribution of all elements in the marine food chain. From shifts in lobster habitat to the rate of phytoplankton growth, from paths of migrating species to more fertile feeding grounds, or moving north to south, south to north, feeding and birthing their young along both coasts of the United States, the sun affects a seasonal pattern invisible to us except for an occasional sighting of a distant spout or diving tail.

In Reykjavik, Iceland, at a meeting of The Arctic Council, I attended a session sponsored by the Government of Brazil, advocating for a membership in that international association of nations with direct Arctic interests. I asked for the rationale behind this application. The answer was an example of econo-political "gathering in", a continuity of fish migrating thousands of miles from southern Brazilian waters to the distant north, providing Brazil with its arguable claim of direct Arctic interest and access to rich Arctic waters.

Such changes affect the opening and closing of fishing seasons. Lobstering in Maine shuts down just as lobstering in Nova Scotia opens up. When the scallop season begins in Maine, I buy them, hand caught and as fresh as any shellfish can be, from the fisherman down the road in buckets to freeze in servings that extend well into the coming spring, even early summer. When it is time to prepare my raised beds for the Maine over-winter, I fill my truck from seaweed wrack on the beach by my town dock. Gathering in.

All this is subtle change that informs a way of being that speaks directly to our health and wellness. Nature shifts and changes throughout the year, differently in every place, but with similar fecundity and substance. As we walk the autumnal fields and observe the changing, falling leaves, we understand that there is a natural order evident, a rotation of goods and services that the farmers know, that the bears and turkeys know, that we don't know so well, or have forgotten.

I speak often of the sustenance the ocean provides – not just the food we eat, but also what we feed our souls. Everywhere on earth, we are drawn to the ocean, not only for physical nurture, but also for its dynamic shifts of color and light, the wind and rain and fog and snow, the force of the natural world that is there for us to harvest – carefully and well – to feed ourselves, literally and socially, to give us strength, meaning, and hope for the future.

We need to listen more often, more clearly, to those poets and writers, to Rob McCall and all my other neighbors who share this ocean community. When the world is fraught with conflict and separation, with argument and scorn, with the decline of civility and civilization, we must pay attention, welcome, and sustain the best of who we are, by gathering in.

CULTURE, CONNECTION AND THE TRANS-ATLANTIC SLAVE TRADE

There is but one ocean, perceived historically as a surface for exploration, transport, and trade, all factors in the making of civilization worldwide. Below that surface lies the detritus of the dangerous endeavor of voyaging: loss by storm, warfare, and ignorance of such a dynamic and challenging environment. That ocean has enabled connection for all time, and has built, through the exchange of knowledge, skills, and traditions, a vast world culture.

One of the most tragic illustrations of this process is the buying and selling of slaves from Africa to the west, South and North America primarily, as cheap, dispensable labor. In the United States, there are there three major contributions to our cultural identity: the existing culture of native peoples living here for centuries; the ensuing

European culture transferred through waves of immigration from England, Ireland, Scotland, and the continent; and the arrival of African culture through slaves that changed our nation's patterns of settlement, music, and language in powerful, undeniable ways. Indigenous people, European people, African people – we are an amalgam of acculturation that lies at the heart of who we are.

We must never allow that fact, and those memories, to be lost, and to guard against such forgetfulness, we turn to material culture – the objects, sites, and other evidence of such history as our foremost tool for preservation. That commitment, evinced by museums, libraries, archives, cultural sites, and national and international organizations such as UNESCO, is an essential part of an endeavor to conserve and honor this collective past in all its forms and manifestations.

In 2019, following the effect of a powerful storm and flood in a muddy riverbank near Mobile, Alabama, remains were revealed of what is purported to be the last ship to transport African slaves to the United States. Researchers claim that the ship may well be the Clotilda, built in the 1850s as a transport for supplies from Cuba, purchased by a local businessman, and commissioned to purchase 110 slaves in Ouimah, a port town in the present-day African nation of Benin. While slavery was then legal in the state of Alabama, the ship's purpose was in violation of US federal law outlawing the slave trade some 52 years before. If the vessel is, indeed, Clotilda, it represents an end – the last shipment of slaves – but also a beginning: the survivors of that ship are reported to have formed a nearby community, called Africa Town, in the middle of the American deep south on the verge of the Civil War. Who knows where the ancestors of those men and women are now?

At the 2017 opening of the Smithsonian National Museum of African American History and Culture, artifacts from another slave ship, the Portuguese *São José-Paquete de Africa* – wrecked of the coast of Cape Town, South Africa, in 1794, en route to Brazil from Mozambique carrying 400 people – were displayed as unique remnants memorializing the maritime aspect of the slave trade. Included was a 200-year-old iron ingot used as ballast and a pulley block, "thought to be [one of] the first objects to be recovered from a slave ship that went down while it was transporting [enslaved] people". The objects were on a 10–year loan to the museum, and their conservation had been partially funded by the US Ambassadors Fund for Cultural Preservation, a program of the Cultural Affairs Office of the US Department of State. The grant of $500,000 had been designated in 2016 by the American Ambassador, through the Bureau of Educational and Cultural Affairs, as recognition of the importance of these artifacts as symbols of the unifying cultural relationship inherent in the vast interconnected history of the trans-Atlantic slave trade.

There is odd correspondence and symmetry in these examples: Africa and the United States, first and last, as if the story begins and ends at extremes, encompassing a story in which lies past, present, and future implication. The consequence of the slave trade is with us still: racism is not lost to history; it extends to, and resonates with, our daily lives. The cry of "black lives matter" is an echo of ballast iron and wooden pulley, of the beams of ships lost and found. The continuity of history carries on through cultural preservation; this is how memory endures. The implications of acculturation cannot be, like the power of an ocean storm, denied. There is wreckage there – disconnection – real, sad, and final.

THE SLAVE ROUTE

Slavery remains a source of basic injustice worldwide. It is an ocean story, a demonstration of exchange, humans as a commodity in international maritime trade. The Trans-Atlantic story demonstrates a "triangular" system of connection across the seas, from Africa to the Americas to raise crops such as sugar and tobacco traded to England and Europe from which manufactured goods were traded back to Africa in a cycle of finance based on enslaved labor that fostered death, brutality, and the shaping of values that have passed down as the foundation for political strife, racial discrimination, continuing contemporary inequality and injustice. Sadly, it is a first manifestation of what we today call globalization.

But the Trans-Atlantic story is but one of three, the others evident in the Indian Ocean and the Middle East and Asia. The United Nations Educational, Scientific and Cultural Organization (UNESCO) has documented these histories in a project call "The Slave Route," an inventory of "memory," of places and events "to assist in providing a better understanding of the causes, forms of operation, issues and consequences of slavery in the world, to present global transformations and cultural interactions that have resulted from this history, and to contribute to a culture of peace by promoting reflection on cultural pluralism, intercultural dialogue, and the construction of new identities and citizenships." Sites memorializing this history have been designated in the United States, United Kingdom, France, Cuba, Guadeloupe, Nigeria, Turks and Caicos, Barbados, and Jamaica, and Peru. There are many more, and one hopes that today's growing awareness and response to endemic racism and its history will provide impetus for many more.

We often consider slavery in the context of colonization, and indeed "colonizers" – primarily American, English, Dutch, and Portuguese – were complicit, procuring human "goods" by purchase, dislocation by local calamity, and internal rebellion or tribal conflict. There was a market, internal supply for external demand, all of it tragic, rationalized by circumstance, immoral, and deadly. But it is clear that labor for the exploitation of resources available through colonial outposts connected by trans-ocean connection was a transformational economic enterprise with far-reaching social consequence that continues to this day.

There are, of course, modern examples of slavery: specifically, in illegal labor migration and human rights abuse and trafficking, primarily of women and children in the context of the trade of drugs and sex workers. Consider the definition of such conduct: "the recruitment, transportation, transfer, harboring, and receipt of persons, by means of threat or use of force or other forms of coercion, of abduction, of fraud, or deception or benefits to achieve the consent of a person having control over another person, for the purpose of exploitation." There are sordid, overt examples: a shipping container discovered with impoverished refugees to be smuggled into a country illegally without security or standing beyond the power of their recruiters, their masters. They can be revealed or traded or disappeared as chattel at any time at the convenience of their owners.

But there are other, more covert, ways to enslave: to provide illegal documents, to under-pay for hard labor rendered, to delimit living conditions and finances, to hold such power as leverage against escape, self-improvement, advancement, and freedom. The threat of deportation and return to tyrannical origins, sweat shops, menial and transient work opportunities, wage scales untenable for basic survival, educational and employment bias, segregated communities of impoverished and working poor, visa and citizenship policies, voter discrimination, racial profiling by police, and the innumerable incidents of subtle, and not so subtle prejudice felt every day, mostly by people of color, the daughters and sons of the slaved at the hands of the sons and daughters of the slavers. Inherent in this is more than an itinerary of historical place and event, but also a passage of historical responsibility, accountability, understanding, and reparation.

We will drown in the turbulent sea of injustice. No one really survives without intervention by virtue of personal or collective will to do so. Injustice knows no limits unless it is resolved by redress and change. Immorality can only be combated by the affirmation of morality. A context of amorality, or indifference, or inaction, will not fease.

It is an ocean story, and we are adrift.

DIVING WITH A PURPOSE

In our oceanic world, culture admixes, and race becomes an undeniable thread of discrimination, brutality, suffering, and death. The forces endure, shifting like a current, with real consequence. Slavery, in all its forms over time, continues, directly as with some fishers and crew on the high seas, or in racially isolated neighborhood, workplace, education, health, and social interaction. As we struggle with the facts, the responsibility, and the solutions, we look for examples where race matters, where cultural equality is affirmed, where real lessons are discovered, and where we find models that might serve to answer, in part, the larger question of how can equality and justice be served.

Diving with a Purpose (DWP) describes itself as "an organization dedicated to the conservation and protection of submerged heritage resources by providing education, training, certification and field experience to adults and youth in the fields of maritime archaeology and ocean conservation. Our special focus is the protection, documentation and interpretation of African slave trade shipwrecks and the maritime history and culture of African-Americans who formed a core of labor and expertise for America's maritime enterprises."

Founded by professional diver, Ken Stewart, "DWP is a volunteer underwater archaeology program that started with members of the National Association of Black Scuba Divers (NABS) and the National Park Service (NPS) in Biscayne National Park. Biscayne National Park is the largest marine park in the National Parks System and has over 110 archaeological sites, approximately 43 of which are intact shipwrecks, that tell compelling stories of the nation's rich maritime cultural heritage."

DWP trains experienced divers, including youth, to become underwater archaeology advocates. Through the program, divers are able to assist in the historical documentation and preservation of artifacts and wreck sites. The program also attempts to interpret and understand the historical context in which the ships existed. As of this writing, more than 300 divers have completed the course and more than 46 have become instructors.

DWP has expanded internationally, beyond the Park's boundaries, with expeditions and training abroad. George Washington University, Smithsonian's Museum of African American History and Culture, South Africa's Iziko Museums and DWP, in partnership, formed the Slave Wrecks Project to search for slave shipwrecks around the globe. In addition:

- DWP has collaborated with the National Oceanic and Atmospheric Administration (NOAA) providing Nautical Archaeology Society (NAS) training and expeditions in the National Marine Sanctuaries. NABS and NOAA have created a website called Voyage to Discovery, which is a multimedia educational initiative highlighting African-American contributions to the country's maritime heritage.
- DWP graduates have recently assisted NOAA with the identification and mapping of the shipwreck *Hannah Bell* in Key Largo and the documentation of a lost Tuskegee Airmen P-39 aircraft in Lake Huron.
- DWP has participated in the search for the *Guerrero*, a pirate slave ship sunk off the coast of Florida, which was featured on an episode called "Sunken Stories" in the PBS Changing Seas documentary series.
- DWP established a Youth DWP archaeology program and has added a Coral Restoration course.

This is an impressive record for any organization. But, let me say this: in my two decades as director of a major American maritime history museum, with a direct involvement in the evolution of nautical archaeology in the United States and similar development of cultural policy abroad, I have never seen an African archeologist or diver at any meeting, on any committee, or otherwise involved in any discussion, direct investigation, best practice and treaty drafts, or anything else associated with the discipline of nautical archaeology. It has been simply that the investigation of African nautical heritage was the purview of non-African scholars and divers: exclusion de facto, call it otherwise what you will. Extend over time and place; extrapolate into hiring practice, scholarship awards, faculty appointments, expedition crews, and museum professionals; amplify to the larger social context in which we live, unmixed; and you see revealed the perpetuation of segregation by race from within the genteel order of cultural history and may understand better the anger and disorder in the streets, no longer invisible unless one is determined not to see.

So, hurrah for Ken Stewart! And for Diving with a Purpose. Agents of integration and reparation within the sea of history that connects all things. What has happened here is the taking back, the recovery of an event, object, its conservation, interpretation, celebration, memory, and strategy for revised cultural understanding of a thing, place, and time that is authentic, personal, communal, and transcendent. For us to truly understand any story, we need the right tellers of the tale to recover what is submerged, bring it to the surface and the light, to shape the narrative correctly: and that is a strategy beyond whatever lies nearly forgotten on the ocean floor, a purpose for the future.

AMISTAD AMERICA: REPARATION

La Amistad, ironically Spanish for "friendship," was a 19th century schooner engaged in the slave trade, transporting human cargo, Mende people, from Sierra Leone to Cuba for work on the Spanish-owned sugar plantations. In 1839, with 53 slaves aboard, these imprisoned passengers revolted, under the leadership of Singbe Pieh, also known as Joseph Cinque, taking command of the ship, killing the captain, with the intent to return to Africa. However, the owners, aboard, set course north up the Atlantic coast of the United States, hopefully to be captured there and returned to Cuba. The ship was taken by a US revenue cutter off Montauk, Long Island, New

York; the slaves nonetheless escaped but were retaken on land and placed in prison in New Haven, Connecticut, and tried on charges of murder and piracy. The ensuing legal battle focused both on property and its return to owners in Cuba, and charges against those owners for the illegal enslavement of Africans. The case was known as *The United States vs The Amistad* (1841) and found its way to the US Supreme Court where the Mende prevailed, exonerated for having rebelled in self-defense, and were restored their freedom.

Forty-three returned to Africa in 1842, aided by the United Missionary Society, led by James W.C. Pennington, a Congregationalist minister and former fugitive slave, active in the abolitionist movement. The Amistad incident became a rallying cry for emancipation and justice in the fight against slavery worldwide.

In that spirit, over 150 years later, a replica of *La Amistad* was constructed, a modern replica intended to sail as an evocation of that history, its memorialization, and its educational potential to continue an international conversation about slavery and its subsequent impact on African-Americans, past, present and future. Funds were raised, much of it from black church organizations, and voyaging commenced to port cities in the name of public outreach and celebration of African culture. Under the direction of a non-profit, Amistad America, the schooner made an extensive passage along the Atlantic coast and an astonishing return to England and then to Sierra Leone in commemoration of the 200th anniversary of the abolition of the slave trade in Britain in 1807, during which the crew broadcast live to the United Nations General Assembly from a point at sea halfway along the route of the "middle passage." To my thinking, that unpublicized event, linking the iconic ship and crew to the global community, was the single most dramatic moment in what thereafter became a second part of the tragedy, with the ensuing confusion over finance, governance, and viability of the original intent as the result of internal politics, funding crises, jurisdictional rivalry, maintenance and operational issues, and decline as a vital symbol and tool for the ongoing discussion of slavery and its consequence in the United States. The vessel now resides at the Mystic Seaport Museum, where she was built, now an educational exhibit with a modest voyaging program, future unknown.

In the world of maritime heritage, replica ships, typically conceived by enthusiasm for the anniversary of historical events, have not had a successful history. Some were built by civic organizations or museums as displays central to their specific history. Others – several sets of the Columbus' ships for example – have succeeded initially and then found declining interest ashore thereafter to the point of abandonment, re-purpose, even destruction. Initially, the *Amistad* and its inaugural voyages captured the imagination of African-Americans, and events at first ports of call were enthusiastically promoted and attended by the community as a celebration and educational impetus for discussion and remembrance. Why the ensuing decline is a complicated story, but one underlying element is the uncertainty of management and finance more and more reliant on government and philanthropy that had interests and agendas other than slavery and its relevance to their other suddenly more pressing interests. Even some in the African American community objected and did not participate, viewing Amistad as counter-symbolic to improvement of race relations and integration, indeed an evocation of a history willfully to be forgotten.

All of us, regardless of origin or history, require icons upon which to focus our memories and our aspirations. As we are challenged to face issues of race in the United States, *Amistad* retains its meaning as "friendship," and remains a powerful tool, not just of its particular event in its particular time, but more importantly as a symbol for freedom, for justice, for equality, and for integrated understanding of how to succeed as a community of "we, the people." What if *Amistad* could re-launch as a symbol of reparation, "the making of amends," around which all Americans might gather to discuss why and how we might resolve what separates us on a voyage of rebuilding and renewal, with all the skills and collaboration required to sail a ship, with the specific navigational way points required to get successfully to a new destination?

THE OCEAN AND FREEDOM

The ocean is freedom. It has, at least until now, the capacity to assimilate, dissolve, nurture, and heal. As we deal with the dual pandemic of virus and racism, the ocean can serve the admixture of intelligence and culture, and of resolve and action. There are the processes of Nature evident therein that can serve as models for our response to past and present social and political disruption and for initiatives by which to guide our way forward.

Slavery was, and remains, a brutal form of appropriation. It captures both body and soul, enforces the tyranny of one world view upon another, demeans the human spirit, and compromises the best of civil society. Colonization, with its appropriation of land and culture, was not limited to the United States, and was imposed upon many other peoples in many other places around the world: India, Asia, South America, and Africa, where foreign nations assumed control of property, law, policy, education, and political order. The imposition of an alien world view imposed on indigenous communities subverted their language, ritual, art, stories of origin, and systems of value. The enforcement of that imposition found expression as regulation, segregation, assimilation, and brutality. If you understand this history, it is no surprise that today we find ourselves faced with protest and resistance, rebellion in the streets and at the ballot box, with disruption amplified by pandemic disease that lays yet another inequitable consequence on people of color.

Protest by black and indigenous voices, and all others affected by such enslavement, must be heard as justifiable anger, resilience, and demand for a just society. I say this as a confession of personal complicity and as a personal resolve to use the ocean as a prospect to be realized, a community of *Citizens of the Ocean* that mimics the integration, dynamism, and healing nature of a world united, not separated, by the sea. Each of us will chose whatever way serves this prospect best.

How do we get beyond the symbolism to the reality? How do we shape our behavior to attempt redress? How does our content change in response to such resolve? How do we reach audience disenfranchised by the system? How do we promote and connect with the ocean community to contribute to such change?

Here are two examples of projects that the World Ocean Observatory has attempted to advance to this end in Africa by promotion, connection, and endorsement:

First, *A Schoolteacher's Guide to Marine Environmental Education in the Eastern African Region* in Tanzania, a full curriculum, developed by African middle school teachers, that presents basic marine science in a specifically African environment, using illustrations of Africans at work in maritime endeavor, local coastal features and systems, and examples of familiar African experience. Second, the Pan African Vision for the Environment in Nigeria, an attempt to create a coalition of schools, organizations, and professional educators across Africa to train teachers to use the curriculum cited above.

Success here can only be achieved by Africans themselves, and our search for sponsorship is ironic as foreign validation of two excellent home-initiated projects to advance marine environmental education in African schools.

In the United States, our focus is on the development of a virtual aquarium and expedition experience accessible to any student at any age anywhere on any device at no cost. The concept here is limited for now only by its presentation in English; otherwise the purpose is to remove all barriers to knowledge such as cost, administrative resistance, teacher resistance, location, ethnic origin, or citizenship, and provide access to a curriculum based on the principles of Ocean Literacy to formal classrooms, informal educational organizations, home-schooling parents, and curious individuals. It is a sad circumstance that the Covid pandemic has raised the potential for this service exponentially.

None of us can do it all. But we can immerse ourselves in the ebb and flow. The challenge is to come out of our present circumstance as if cleansed and re-directed. To swim in the ocean is one thing, to come safely ashore through current and wave is another. We are on the edge. We will be submerged and rolled. There will be sand in our eyes and seaweed in our hair. We will lie on the sand, exhilarated and free.

UNDERWATER CULTURAL HERITAGE

By 2009, the UNESCO Convention on the Protection of Underwater Cultural Heritage had been ratified by twenty nations since its publication in 2001. The Convention establishes standards and guidelines for the survey of sites and the recovery of artifacts classified as cultural relics, and defines protections against salvage operations within waters of national jurisdiction until appropriate research and archeological investigations can take place. However, most of the nations that have officially ratified the convention are small island nations. Of countries in the industrialized world, only Spain, Portugal, and Mexico are listed; the United States and Canada, most of Europe, South America, and the Far East are conspicuously absent.

This does not mean that these nations have not created their own system of protections. The US has allocated responsibility to the individual states, which have created their own structures to oversee administration, survey, and recovery. Australia, New Zealand, Japan, and the European Union all have policy and legal frameworks in place, as do many other nations, such as the Philippines and China. Still, these nations have not signed on to the international convention; just as many of them, such as the United States, have not yet ratified the related United Nations Convention on the Law of the Sea. A conference of ocean leaders in Washington, DC, provided some hope that the American administration would address the situation through the approval of a new national ocean policy as recommended by two commissions and the ocean caucus in the US Congress.

The convention was the result of numerous examples of destruction of submerged cultural resources in the 1980s and '90s by salvage operations and zealous treasure hunters. Perhaps the most notorious of these was the discovery of the *Atocha*, a Spanish galleon, by salvor Mel Fisher, and the indiscriminate recovery of artifacts from the *Titanic*. Cultural protection organizations such as the Council of American Maritime Museums, the International Congress of Maritime Museums, and UNESCO, countered with proposed protections that have subsequently been the basis for state regulations, national laws, and, eventually, the international treaty.

Important discoveries continue to be made as the result of the exploration of the deep ocean by commercial interests and syndicates of investors looking for lost cargoes of Chinese porcelain, pay-ship bullion, and artifacts of value in the cultural market. In the southern Mediterranean Sea in 2007, a marine survey expedition for a proposed gas pipe-line monitored a sonar target that, upon further investigation, was identified as the French battleship *Danton*, built in Brest in 1910 and sunk in 1917. The ship, claimed by the French as both naval property and a grave site, was extensively documented by photographs and video, and the gas-line was offset to leave the artifact undisturbed and available for future inquiry. More recently, *HMS Victory*, a Royal Navy warship that was the precursor to the more famous flagship of Admiral Horatio Nelson, was discovered more than 100 kilometers from the site off the Channel Islands where, in 1774, she was lost with all hands, foundering on a reef. In this case, the search was conducted under a cooperative agreement with UK Ministry of Defense mandating extensive archaeological investigation and control.

The shipwreck had been extensively damaged by natural deterioration, scouring, and bottom trawls in an area heavily fished by commercial vessels. What remains, however, is a complete set of bronze cannons, including a 42-pounder, the only known example of a gun of this size in existence, which will be recovered, no doubt, for display in a naval museum.

SACRED PLACES

Let us think of renewal, of beginnings, rather than ends, hopes instead of fears. For many, the traditions of formal religions provide the words and order of these preoccupations; for others, private thoughts and special places provide. In each of these, Nature plays some part – as allegory, animation of the divine, or sacred spaces where we find the source and strength for the future.

Many such spaces exist along the shore throughout the world, as evidence of complex, intangible relationship between us and our originating web of life. The ocean itself is frequently invoked for its emotional depth and dynamic breadth as a metaphor for freedom from life's burdens and tyrannies and for opportunity for passage into the future.

In a collection of essays titled *Sacred Natural Sites, Conserving Nature & Culture* (Earthscan, 2010), the Editors discuss this phenomenon worldwide. Among many examples, islands hold special meaning – Lindisfarne Island, for instance, since 635 AD has been a holy site for Christian pilgrimage linking nature and spirituality. Located on the northeast coast of England at the Scottish border, Lindisfarne is surrounded by rich wetlands, and is accessible only at low tide, across sand and mud flats marked by an ancient pilgrim's path and a modern causeway. Today, it is home to a resident community of 150, with up to half a million visitors per year, who come a place that housed Christian monastic communities and nurtured the lives of saints for centuries. Primary among them is St. Cuthbert, considered "one of the most important saints of Medieval England and Europe," whose affinity for nature, seabirds, and the protection of wildlife and wild places foreshadowed the modern conservation movement.

In the Philippines, on Coron Island, off Palawan, the indigenous Calamian Tagbanwa people have defined ten sacred areas in the sea where they believe divine spirits dwell, which must be protected as sanctuaries from which fishing, dropping of anchors, or culturing seaweed are prohibited. These sites can only be entered by shamans, elders, and worshipers, whose prayers name and invoke the wide variety of marine species and natural physical characteristics of the areas, thereby connecting spiritual beliefs with natural phenomenon through unique personal and community religious practice.

Such places have found allies in the biodiversity protection movement and associated governance designed to conserve the fulsome catalogue of species and habitat typically coexisting with sacred spaces. Research studies, management practices, legal instruments, education and training projects abound, justifying protections, providing models and international conventions, and establishing communications and enforcement methods that meet the goals of both theist and conservationist.

On what premises is this unexpected coalition based? First, there is a real and widespread interconnection between sacred spaces and bio-diverse areas around the world. Second, the degradation of one threatens the integrity of the other, and these degradations are accelerating and destructive to the value of both. Third, faith, spirituality, and science are complementary ways of understanding human-to-Nature relationships, and the protection of places in which all three intersect can be seen as a means to sustain ecologically sound ways of life. And, fourth, by virtue of these premises, a strategy to build public awareness and supportive policies and laws is worthwhile and urgently needed.

Should we not all have such places – a river or lake to sit by, a beach to walk, a space in which to reflect and renew and connect with all things sacred?

INTANGIBLE CULTURAL HERITAGE

"Heritage" refers to practices or characteristics that are passed down from one generation to the next. I may have long misunderstood the definition, conditioned to think that heritage is embodied only in places and things – in castles, chateaux, churches, and monuments, in paintings, drawings, objects, and other physical remnants associated with the great events, institutions, and movements in our history. Frequently, we lament the loss of such last great places, or endangered spaces wherein defining elements of our civilization took place.

The United Nations Educational, Scientific, and Cultural Organization (UNESCO) is the international agency charged with identification and protection of such places through its World Heritage Site designation, a list of monuments and cultural remnants considered the most important worldwide. To see all these places in a lifetime would be an education worthy of the time, energy, and cost of getting there.

There is a second designation of "intangible cultural heritage," defined by the UNESCO Convention as "the practices, representations, expressions, knowledge, skills – as well as the instruments, objects, artifacts and cultural spaces associated therewith – that communities, groups and, in some cases, individuals recognize as part of their cultural heritage. This intangible cultural heritage, transmitted from generation to generation, is constantly recreated by communities and groups in response to their environment, their interaction with Nature and their history… (in the form of) oral traditions and expressions; performing arts; social practices, rituals and festive events; knowledge and practices concerning nature and the universe; and traditional craftsmanship."

Here are the four ocean-related practices, paraphrased from their UNESCO descriptions:

1. In Belgium, "twelve households in Oostduinkerke actively engage in shrimp fishing, using Brabant draft horses, walking breast-deep in the surf, parallel to the coastline, pulling hand-woven funnel-shaped nets held open by two wooden boards, with an attached chain dragged over the sand to create vibrations, causing the shrimp to jump into the net to be emptied into baskets hanging at the horses' sides.

The event takes place twice a week, except in the winter months, and culminates in a two-day Shrimp Festival for which the local community spends months building floats, making costumes, preparing street theatre, and introducing shrimp catching to over 10,000 visitors every year."

2. In Iran, "Lenj vessels are traditionally hand-built and are used by inhabitants of the northern coast of the Persian Gulf for sea journeys, trading, fishing and pearl diving. The traditional knowledge surrounding Lenjes includes oral literature, performing arts and festivals, sailing and navigation techniques and terminology, weather forecasting, and wooden boatbuilding. Iranian navigators could locate the ship according to the positions of the sun, moon and stars, using special formulae to calculate latitudes and longitudes, and special vocabulary to estimate water depth, type of wind, and the characteristics of approaching weather."

3. In Mali, "the Sanké mon collective fishing rite takes place in San in the Ségou region every second Thursday of the seventh lunar month to commemorate the founding of the town. The rite begins with the sacrifice of roosters, goats and offerings made by village residents to the water spirits of the Sanké pond. The collective fishing then takes place over fifteen hours using large and small mesh fishing nets, followed by a masked dance on the public square featuring Buwa dancers from San and neighboring villages, who wear traditional costumes and hats decorated with cowrie shells and feathers, and perform specific choreography to the rhythms of a variety of drums."

4. In China, "beginning on the fifth day of the fifth lunar month, people of several ethnic groups throughout China and the world celebrate the Dragon Boat festival. The festivities vary from region to region, but they usually include a memorial ceremony offering sacrifices to a local hero combined with such sporting events as dragon races, dragon boating and willow shooting; feasts of rice dumplings, eggs and ruby sulfur wine; and folk entertainments including opera, song and unicorn dances."

Each of these events, and more than 200 more on the list, strengthens the tangible bonds between the participants, families, neighbors, and visitors. Each is based on the harmonious relationship between humanity and nature, individual imagination and collective creativity, identity and continuity, community and cultural diversity – revealing, conserving, and communicating a vivid sense of cultural identity that we can see, touch, feel, and celebrate.

MOTTAINAI!

The Japanese have long engaged in concepts that somehow resonate and shape my thoughts about how to live in this world. *In Praise of Shadows*, a telling essay on Japanese aesthetics by Junichiro Tanizaki, awarded the 1958 Nobel Prize for Literature, describes the appreciation of that ephemeral space where light meets dark, where bright contradictions give way to an inarticulate aura that is both complicated and simple, a dusky reconciliation of forces or ideas, a place where illusive harmony may be found if you are open to looking for it.

Wabi-Sabi is another such concept: the value of a patina of use found in Nature, in abandoned places, and in artistic traditions, raised to an aesthetic transcendence that resonates and inspires appreciation for the elegance of utility and its meaning. These insights have purpose for defense against the raucous, unrelenting chaos of modern life. In Zen meditation, in adherence to tradition in the face of accelerating change, is the search for an alternative set of values to inform and manifest a different future.

The ocean represents such a healing space. It is a constant presentation of motion and light, a theater of sight and sound and feeling that draws us to and into it, for re-creation in every sense of that word and activity. Why do we continue to migrate to the coast the world over, which soothes and lifts our spirits, even if we don't know why?

There is another Japanese term that pertains: *Mottainai*, derived from a Buddhist term that referred to the essence of things. In a catalogue essay titled *Mottainai: The Fabric of Life*, for an exhibition of traditional Japanese textiles at the Portland Japanese Garden in Oregon, USA, Curator Diane Durston writes, "Applied to everything in the physical universe, the word suggests that objects do not exist in isolation but are intrinsically linked to one another. *Nai* is a negation, so *mottainai* is an expression of sadness for the disrespect shown when any living or non-living entity is wasted.

"Mottainai!" parents say, admonishing their children not to waste a single scrap of paper. In a land where natural resources have always been scarce, people have long understood the importance of respecting the value of all things and of wasting nothing. It was the only way to survive in less affluent times."

Wangari Maathai – founder of the Greenbelt Movement in Africa, democracy advocate and political activist, and winner of the 2004 Nobel Peace Prize – responded to *mottainai* during a visit to Japan. She used the concept as focal point in her call for an international campaign to reduce waste and recycle, which has continued after her death in 2011.

There is another Japanese phrase: *Sato-Umi*, defined thusly: 'Sato' means the area where people live, and "Umi" means the sea. Sato-umi is an important sea area that has been supporting culture and cultural exchanges through such things as fisheries and the distribution of products. It is an area that includes both Nature and human beings, as well as an area in which both high biological productivity and biodiversity are expected. Healthy Sato-umi provides numerous blessings: when the natural circulation function is appropriately maintained, when integrated and comprehensive management of the land and coastal area is performed, and when the rich and diversified ecosystem and natural environment are conserved. This 'preferable coastal area environment' must be maintained with the cooperation of more people in order to accede this precious environment to future generations."

All this conceptual language may describe a new strategy for our relationship with the ocean: a place that reflects the outcome of our use, that respects and sustains the value of Nature, and that integrates and reconciles human needs and natural resources for the future of all mankind. *Mottainai!*

MOKEN

Moken is a Thai word meaning "sea people, people of the water, sea nomads or sea gypsies". It is a term used to describe a group of Austronesian people of the Mergui Archipelago, some 800 islands claimed by both Myanmar and Thailand, their total population comprising less than 3000 people who live and make their living in and on the ocean. It may seem totally primitive to our modern view, but that way of life

contains certain values and behaviors that might be exemplary for us all.
There is a movement afoot for a simpler life: some folks opting out of the consumer
matrix; some defining comfort and safety in different value terms that are not just
romantic or idealistic fantasy, but are another form of modern engagement with land
and sea in the context of sustainability and community.

Where I live, I am surrounded by young farmers and fishers engaged in a new
organic agriculture or the harvest of marine species – gathering and hunting, if you
will – in a simpler world that is not primitive at all. The Moken have accumulated
a vast knowledge of the sea, and while they harvest with spears and nets, dry and
prepare product on the decks of their floating homes, bartering and selling at local
markets, these habits are not so far removed from what occurs in my local farmers'
market of a Saturday throughout the year: farmed meats and dairy, fish and shellfish,
winter vegetables, home-prepared foods, baked goods, sea salt distilled from our
local waters, and other unique products.

The Moken are under extreme pressure from the ever-inflicted government policies
of assimilation, language suppression, re-location, and subversion of cultural
traditions. Why is it that governments fear "the other" with such consistent attempts
to suppress freedom to live apart, with art and tradition that is nothing more
dangerous than a continuity of personal expression and collective belief? We see
it everywhere that minorities dwell, especially when these communities rise up
to protect what is, to them, both worldly and sacred. Look at religious conflict in
Arabia, tribal conflict in Africa and China, racial and ethnic conflict in Europe and
the United States, and you discover the same underlying opposition to diversity and
identity – whether by dictators, monolithic governments, corporate dominance,
religious uniformity, and all the other structures that work, sometimes together,
to oppress, suppress, even eradicate these last vestiges of culture. Why does the
Thai government attempt to re-locate and domesticate the Moken? Look no further
than offshore oil discoveries in the surrounding water by Unocal, Petronas, and
other international energy companies to understand the political pressure for
transportation of the Moken to the alien mainland, – out of sight, out of mind, out of
the way of the environmental impact of drilling and mining and all the other morally
bankrupt financial enterprises, proven so destructive on land and poised to be just as

destructive at sea. If the new definition of civilization is to repeat the corrosive and corrupting behaviors of the past, this small event in a place far away is but another example of that decline.

Various anthropologists and scientists have studied the Moken as some kind of vestigial culture. Moken children see better underwater than European children – a hypothesis theorized and confirmed by a comparative study of physiology and visual acuity by a Swedish scientist. The explanation posited was constriction of pupils and accommodation of visual focus to the specific conditions. Moken children see differently than we do, a behavior conditioned by the circumstances of survival – gathering mollusks, marine plants, and fish for protein. The European children were debilitated by sustained temporary eye irritation underwater, "red eye" that left them blind to the harvest.

Vision: 1) the act or power of sensing with the eyes; 2) the act or power of anticipating that which will or may come to be. Some look at the ocean and see oil and gas; these are the "red-eyed" ones. Others look at the ocean and see community and sustainability; these are the "clear-eyed" ones – sea people, shaped by the past, reacting to the present, and looking at what must soon come to be. We are among them; we are all *Citizens of the Ocean*; we are all people of the water.

WORLD AQUARIA

In 2014, the directors and senior staff of the world's aquariums gathered in Shanghai, China for a quadrennial conference on the state of the industry. More than 750 delegates from over 300 organizations in 45 countries were in attendance to hear presentations on new construction, exhibition design, research projects, techniques for controlled capture of aquarium animals in the deep ocean, and reproduction of aquarium animals through aquaculture and other non-invasive means.

There are over 50 aquariums in China alone. New, very expensive modern aquariums continue to be built – in Atlanta, Georgia, in the United States, in Sharjah, the United Arab Emirates, and Singapore. Unlike museums, many aquariums are owned by for-profit companies, a sub-set of the entertainment industry (for profit organizations such as Sea World and Ocean Park have multiple locations). All present were dealing with changing aspects of the world market: the competition for leisure time and disposable income, the need to evolve from the spectacle of performances to the more comprehensive inclusion of education and research, and the shift toward more active advocacy for ocean sustainability through a collective audience estimated at more than 300 million visitors each year.

Clearly, aquariums were moving toward a more activist conservation approach. The New England Aquarium, for example, reported on active research in a newly created Marine Protected Area in the Phoenix Islands of the western Pacific; the Sunshine International Aquarium in Japan described their attempts to breed and transplant coral; numerous presentations focused on captive breeding of sharks, seahorses, sturgeon, reef fish, and even organisms from deep sea vents for the aquarium trade.

The World Ocean Observatory presented a new concept for the distribution of information and education through a fee-based subscription service that pro-rates the expense of production and distribution of short documentaries, interviews with scientists in the field, project profiles, new links, and educational activities across a global aquarium network at an astonishingly affordable rate. Other programs to expand public awareness of ocean issues included World Ocean Day, held annually on June 8th, and a cooperative campaign to have this event accredited by the United Nations; Ocean Passport, a document to be stamped for visitors at aquariums world-wide; and the active promotion of guides to the purchase and consumption of sustainable seafood in the context of individual human health as well as an effective free-market force against indiscriminate harvest of endangered species. Today, in the context of global pandemic, many of these aquariums are not open to the public.

The potential of aquariums as powerful change agents in expanding public awareness of ocean issues is formidable. Three hundred million visitors have already declared basic interest by program attendance, presenting an enormous opportunity for further education and local citizen action. This is uncharted water for many of these institutions, but it is clear that the mandate was essential to the future success of an industry that is devoted exclusively to a vital and viable ocean.

FISH MARKETS

Wherever I go, I am drawn to fish markets – whether street stalls, neighborhood stores, city markets, or even the counters at supermarkets. I am inevitably attracted by the actuality of such places; the variety, color, strangeness of the species, the fecundity and health implicit in the ocean's bounty, and the special beauty of life, lost life, and life enhanced by gifts from the sea.

Markets are typically animated by fishmongers, often immigrants, who bring to the place a social vitality derived from the old country, recipes and customs, and a certain colorful exchange between workers, customers, and tourists. It amazes me that markets are so lively, even surrounded by catch, paused in waiting, to serve me with life in a wonderful circle of natural reciprocity. Markets also evince the authenticity of work – hard work, dangerous work – by people often far away, in places as foreign as the fish themselves. There is truth there, a challenge by a world so stark and different from the gloss and ease and normality of our privileged lives, so separated and protected from such distant reality. Markets are foreign, nurturing, exciting, connecting – this latter is their very purpose: to connect the world though the beneficence of marine life.

I was, for twenty years, the surrogate landlord for the Fulton Fish Market in New York City. As president of the South Street Seaport Museum and Development Corporation, I oversaw the relationship between the market and city government, a role that required that I work daily with the wholesalers and distributors, loaders and unloaders, to maintain the operational efficiency of a market that was itself an historical artifact. Conceived as a celebration of the maritime contribution to New York and the nation, the Fulton Fish Market was one of the museum's most exciting exhibits. I lived in the Seaport District; the market was right outside my door. My children would pass through in the early morning on their way to school. I would sometimes walk out into the market in the after-midnight hours to experience it, try to understand how it worked, and what it meant for the welfare of a vast urban community that consumed fish in enormous amounts, harvested and distributed from all around the world. I would meet the market leaders at Carmine's, the local bar that catered to their nighttime hours, to discuss problems and changes. It was the end of their workday, and I shared with them steak, eggs and rye; their dinner, my breakfast.

I have visited markets in Lisbon, Portugal; Santiago, Chile; Nuuk, Greenland, and Tokyo, Japan, among many others. The new Toyusu Market in Tokyo – a modern replacement of the very colorful Tsukiji Market – was designed to maximize access, operational utility, and working conditions with new systems, distribution structures, and health conditions. What the old facility boasted in color and historical romance is now transcended by cleanliness, efficiency, and economy.

Still, when you attend the auctions for tuna or sea urchin, the old ways are evident: the mysterious hand-gestures of the bidders, the frantic speed of transaction, and the understood accountability for each transaction. The individual stalls of buyers and sellers are still there, the ancient methods of cutting the fish remain, the perfect beauty of skilled hand and long knife cutting a tuna into perfect, deep red, sculptural sections. The presentation of products has been dramatically modernized with vacuum packaging and aerated containers to protect freshness and transportation, whether to the sushi restaurant next door or the market 3,000 miles away.

In my market in Maine, I found a container of smoked mussels from Japan. I bought them, along with a package of tiny minnow fish, perfectly salted and dried. There is a Japanese saying that when a person looks into a bowl of rice, she sees the shadow of each grain – every grain among thousands. Think about those single mussels and minnows among millions. Where did they come from? How were they caught and processed? How did they find their way from Asian catch to an American table? Each was perfect in itself; like the clarity of those grains of rice, each was once swimming free, only to find its way to my dinner.

It is, by all explanation, inexplicable that one small fish, taken from so far away, is there to serve me, to sustain me, to share with me all the implication of engagement with the sea. Truth is in each single fish everywhere. Each is a gift to us all through an ocean of giving.

WATER CITY

The mighty sound of rain captures my memory; the many variants of water moving through the atmosphere, falling on lakes and streams, down through cascade and rock formations, over dams and through sluices, into backwaters and turning eddies, over sand and stone along the coasts, and amplified to crescendo – breaking water, waves returning from land to sea, breaking around me in the small vessel of my body

I reflect often on the magic of water. Here is an excerpt by Nature writer Annie Dillard, from her wonderful book, *Pilgrim at Tinker Creek*: "It has always been a happy thought to me that the creek runs on all night, new every minute, whether I wish it or know it or care, as a closed book on a shelf continues to whisper to itself its own inexhaustible tale. So many things have been shown so to me on these banks so much light has illumined me by reflection here where the water comes down, that I can hardly believe that this grace never flags, that the pouring from ever renewable sources is endless, impartial, and free."

Flowing water is not limited to the pastoral. It defines major cities like London, Shanghai, and New York. It presents river confluence on which inland cities are built. It outlines the histories of first civilizations, where water flowed in aqueducts, hidden pipes and submerged ponds, and canals built for the distribution of goods, the provision of services, the movement of people from place to place. We know these cities: Venice, St. Petersburg, Amsterdam, Suzhou, Bangkok, et cetera. Many such cities polluted these waterways with manufacturing run-off, toxic and human waste. They were filled and covered over to make streets, while the polluted water was conveyed invisibly through engineered underground tunnels and sewers, to empty into lakes, inlets, and industrial harbors from which the modern city frequently turns away.

Only in recent decades has there been a resurgence of urban waterfront development whereby the rotting, abandoned urban water's edge has been reclaimed – as filled land on which entire new areas of city are constructed or restored as linear parks and recreational facilities, or as expensive high-rise apartment buildings with water views Given the ubiquity and need for water for health and solace, it is hard to believe that the water connection could have been so easily abandoned, now to be expensively recovered as a civic space.

Let us consider Tokyo, a city known for its intense, quirky modernity, an inner-directed hive where people work and play with special abandon. To move through

Tokyo is to submit to its manic system of transportation – subways, trains, congested traffic, effusive sidewalks, under and over passes, and labyrinthine passages that often duplicate the activity on the surface, a second, even third, level of city, illumined artificially with light-marks by which to navigate, and artistic neon that is as sculptural as it is informative.

When we read about Tokyo history, we think of the "floating world," a system of stylized behaviors and formalized structures that express the special cultural identity of Japan. We think of *ukiyo-e* woodblocks prints of ladies and gentlemen in bright kimono, smiling and whispering behind their fans, reading and writing poetry, and engaged in political and romantic intrigue in a watery world of manners, expectations, and traditions.

I discovered that this modern Tokyo hides a neglected, seemingly forgotten, network of rivers – the Arakawa, Sumidagawa, Edogawa, and Tamagawa, and over 100 natural streams and man-made canals – that wind, often invisibly through springs, ponds, hollows and hills, reservoirs, parks and neighborhoods, to which residents have been long indifferent as a coherent, integrated element in the urban topography. A group of passionate urban historians called *Suribachi Gakkai* are engaged in advocacy, planning, and public communication toward the restoration of the old waterways as the physical embodiment of memory and a pastoral softening of the hard edges of Tokyo city life. And so the revival begins. I intend to take part, having found a guide to show me by kayak through this vestigial labyrinth of water-ways and by-ways that once were the circulating force of Tokyo, the water city. I intend to paddle quietly in the great noisy city and to listen for the water, for the grace that never flags, that "pouring from ever renewable sources (that) is endless, impartial, and free."

CITY OF CONNECTION

I went to Istanbul, Turkey, with an assignment from *WoodenBoat Magazine*, an American publication that, over the past forty years, has inspired and documented a vital revival of indigenous small craft, associated construction methods, and an international audience for maritime tradition. I proposed to explore the maritime heritage of the city and to document its present-day condition. In advance, I contacted curators at two maritime museums, The Naval Museum and the Koc Museum of Transportation, each charged with the interpretation of Turkish maritime history, be it the Ottoman Navy or the small craft and maritime trades of the region. To my dismay, both curators demurred when it came to advice as to where I might find historic vessels, restoration projects, or new wooden boat shipyards, places where a modern iteration of heritage skills might be revealed. Such things exist certainly in the United States and in Europe – boat shops, schools, enthusiast associations, marine festivals, replicas, and educational programs on land and sea that preserve and promote the history, skills, and values of national or regional patrimony. Surely, my counselors were wrong; surely such things must exist. Not so: it was not to be as I imagined.

Istanbul does not disappoint on any front – it is an astonishing city, at that moment in fulsome growth, with a burgeoning economy, a palpable sense of optimism, a pending application to join the European Union, a secular government (albeit one now grappling with the same tumultuous religious, social, and autocratic political forces that seriously conflict within all nations of the Middle East). There was a border altercation with Syria underway during my visit; city life seemed outwardly unconcerned, but conversations revealed a nervous questioning as to motivation, escalation, and potential impact on the status quo. My visits to mosques and museums, churches, bazaars, cultural events, and restaurants seemed distanced from the situation, protected within the patterns of touristic behavior.

What became apparent, however, was that, despite my preconceptions, I felt as powerful an evocation of things maritime as I have known anywhere else – not New York, not San Francisco, not Rotterdam, not Hong Kong, not Sidney, not Shanghai – all cities that heretofore I have numbered as the most sea-connected places of modern times. Istanbul did not need history; it did not need a re-birth driven by nostalgia; it had built into its geography, environment, transportation system, economy, and recreation – indeed, into every aspect of its daily life, indeed, into its very soul – a direct, visceral connection to the sea.

The city is aligned along three bodies of water: the Black Sea to the north, and the Bosporus as a channel to the Sea of Marmara to the south. Thus, an axis is established that enables an extraordinary progress of marine transportation: some 300 ships daily, a tanker or freighter every five minutes, 24 hours a day, carrying import and export from and to Russia, Bulgaria, Romania, Ukraine, and Georgia through to the Mediterranean Sea, the Atlantic Ocean, and the world. Surely the Bosporus is one of the most strategic connections extant, like the Suez and Panama Canals, and other key straits through which an enormous volume of seaborne trade must pass.

There is a second axis, east to west across the Bosporus, connecting the European side of the city to the Asian side, to the vast Anatolian plain of Turkey, and on to Syria, Iraq, Iran, and the nations beyond. This connection, too, is primarily marine – a contradictory flow of ferries, excursion vessels, small transports, support vessels, private yachts, local fish boats, and more – diametrically crossing the line of the first axis in equally dense patterns of activity. It is apparent chaos. Yes, there are pilots aboard the larger ships; yes, there is a series of radar towers and a few cursory aids to navigation; but the appearance is of disorder from which, by daily miracle, each vessel reaches its destined shore, bow to quay, and from which a torrent of passengers, produce, rugs, chickens and sheep flows against a waiting current of equal volume prepared to board those vessels for immediate return. It never stops. To walk the edges of the city everywhere there is an unavoidable, insistent, sensory experience of the sea.

Istanbul has grown from two million to thirteen million people in two decades. The old city remains intact, but the new population inhabits coastal development as far as the eye can see in every direction. The buildings are high rises, tiered up to the encircling mountains, layered construction that enables an omnipresent panoramic view of the water and the marine activity below, from almost every window. In short, the sea is visible and felt from everywhere.

Comes, then, the question: who needs the past when the present is so visible and vibrant? Who needs retrospection when the present prospect is so pervasive and real? Who needs a renaissance when the reality is so alive and well? Istanbul is a stunning realization of the sea's connections – of goods, people, and ideas, on and across the water, linking our hearts and minds through the ocean.

THE POWER OF INNOVATION

One way to look at the history of technology is as a survey of evolving efficiency – the continuing search through invention and management to aggregate functionality and delivery of its effects as efficiently as possible. Devices and their operating systems are considered ever-expanding, useful tools in the delivery of faster results in time and space. Short-cut technologies are a primary obsession of venture capitalists in their search for the next big thing in our techno-world.

The delivery of energy is a consummate case in point. From a single homesteader cutting firewood or plowing a row, we have progressed to massive generation powered by fossil fuels and distributed by national and international, grids and pipelines that deliver energy to burgeoning population and industrial agriculture and manufacturing that now meet our need to consume, build, and thrive. Under-developed communities look for this scale of energy to provide progress from poverty to prosperity and stability. Developed communities continue to cleave, unlimited, and demand more and more energy from fewer and fewer available conventional sources. This operating system demand, then, requires exponential additional supply, even if it leads to conflict, war, and other unforeseen negative consequence to meet the collective need worldwide. This would seem to describe the situation we face: as our old generating systems decline and pollute, our old plants and grid cannot maintain adequate delivery, and our natural resource supplies peak and dissipate to the point of collapse.

Technology has responded through new, more efficient systems, less reliant on unsustainable supply: the opportunities of hydro, wind, solar, and geo-thermal power that can produce more, cost less, and be distributed more effectively, efficiently, and sustainably for a world that is both bigger and smaller as its population grows.

We are all aware of these alternative energy technologies. We see the ever-increasing number of wind and solar farms, often in surprising places. We see the statistics that indicate that more and more nations and communities are abandoning the expensive and polluting coal production, oil and fracking consumption, and even nuclear generation, which, decades ago, was the great hope for our clean energy future, save for the pesky question of what to do with its toxic radioactive residue. How do we maximize these new efficiencies to even greater effect?

In Germany and other European nations, the Norwegian energy conglomerate Statkraft has begun to implement a new digital market access platform intended to assess the variables of weather, consumer demand, price volatility, disconnected markets, large and small generation sources, and decentralized storage into a single system that allows for independent control of the distribution of power through an integrated, smarter grid to an ever-changing reality of supply and demand. For example, in Germany, Statkraft has created what it calls a "virtual power plant," the first of its kind, that unites production of over 1300 wind farms, 100 solar power producers, 12 biomass power plants, and 8 hydropower projects to centralize the distribution of more than 10,000 megawatts, roughly equivalent to 10 nuclear reactors. The company is currently rolling out similar projects in the United Kingdom, France, and Turkey. Other companies in other regions are following suit.

Shortcuts -- the reduction of energy required to deliver energy, the affirmation of greater efficiency as a desirable and profitable enhancement of greater efficiency, the application of existing technology to amalgamate and amplify the productivity of existing technology – these are simplifying and sustainable solutions that demonstrate the power of invention and innovation. Desalination. Ocean geothermal energy. Saltwater irrigation. Aquaponics. Synthesis of marine genetic material for medicine and food. Such ideas, applied, freed from the inhibition and sabotage of vested, unchanging interests, are the pathways to change and the future. Ocean-generated energy is yet to be technologically achieved at scale, but, when it comes, such systems of distribution will be essential to the success of what will surely be the most dynamic and sustainable energy system on earth.

HEALING WITH FISH

Time and again in history we hear of natural treatments for breaks, wounds, and diseases. Our ancestors brewed herbal teas, treated wounds with moss and leaves, and otherwise practiced a healing system derived from natural materials. The tradition continues in the practice of homeopathic medicine in various forms in both East and West, through the global industry in organic supplements, offering an alternative practice to the synthetic, and expensive, methodology that characterizes the health care system in the United States. As medicine has become standardized and mechanized and arbitrated by the insurance, pharmaceutical, and efficiency-driven practices of our time, we have lost much of that historical wisdom and its healing effect.

I speak often of the innovative and effective inventions and organizations in Iceland, a small country with a big heart, big ideas, and a powerful natural environment that provides not only its energy and food requirements, but also a basis for adaptation and invention of natural products and processes to drive its 21st-century economy and culture.

As Iceland relies heavily on fishing in its mix of finance and labor applications, it must stay competitive against larger, industrialized fishing nations by maximizing the value of its fish products: using 100% of the fish. This seems obvious, but, in the US for example, we waste more than half of each fish by discarding by-catch, harvesting only specialized high-cost species, and failing to capture the added economic opportunity of such limited application and interest.

In an article in *Bloomberg BusinessWeek*, Lois Parshley reports on development of a fish-skin-based, FDA-approved treatment for chronic wounds and inflammation – 100% of the fish, indeed. The only hint of its origin is a scale-like grid that also provides a matrix for binding, around which new, healthy skin can grow.

I had seen this product in Reykjavik; it has subsequently been approved by the US Food and Drug Administration. Called "Omega 3 Wound," the product is produced by Kerecis Limited, a small company located in Isafjordur, a town of 3,000 inhabitants with a limited economy based on fishing and small-scale tourism. According to Fertram Sigurjonsson, CEO of Kerecis, the product took nine years to develop and test successfully, using the skin of cod fish caught locally, cleaned, dried, sterilized, and packaged for treatment of chronic wounds, burns, oral cancer, internal, cosmetic and reconstructive surgeries, and other applications for the reduction of inflammation and pain.

The market implication is large. According to Parshley's article, "Some six and a half million Americans suffer from chronic wounds, whether related to vascular disease, diabetes, or complications from normal procedures. The five-year survival rate is 54%, and treatments cost more than $25 billion a year."

Parshley continues, "The US Department of Defense is on the look-out for better burn treatments because of the increase in service wounds from improvised explosive devices. In a study conducted by the US Army Institute of Surgical Research, the fish skin bested the healing rates of cadaver skin, a common military treatment for burns. The Army has also funded several further studies, showing that unlike rival products, fish skin can ward off bacteria and reduce bleeding."

What we have here is a turning of the circle of knowledge, the re-discovery and re-application of the healing property of fish oil, harvested from a traditional food product, enabling new employment for fishing communities, and innovative, more powerful treatment for the injuries of modern war and of many other conditions that can be healed better and faster by a natural process derived from the ocean.

That is the true message here: the ocean has an enormous, known and unknown, implication for human health. When we fail to use it well – or, worse, when we despoil or exhaust it – we are depriving ourselves and our children from its healing properties; in a simple bandage, a new medicine, or the purity of the food we eat, the water we drink, and the air we breathe. The sea connects all things.

INVENTING FISH

We are all aware of the crisis in world fisheries that has brought many species to the verge of extinction. Fishing is big business. According to a Hamilton Project report based on US National Marine Fisheries Service statistics, fishing in the US represents some $90 billion in annual revenues and supports over one and half million jobs.

NOAA classifies 17% of US fisheries as "overfished," and resource management schemes, applied by zones and species, are at the center of an industry response to this serious natural resource challenge.

What is astonishing is that, beyond national catch, an estimated 94% of seafood consumed in the United States is imported from foreign suppliers. In reality, American demand is up, national supply is inadequate, and foreign fishers, often operating without harvest limits, are providing an enormous majority of the product we eat. The paradox is obvious: whatever we do to sustain the national industry will be countered by external suppliers operating outside sustainability management regimes to meet an ever-growing market demand.

Historically, management regulations were established by permits for controlled entry into area waters, limited season lengths, and catch quotas – procedures that have proven controversial and inadequate. A new approach, called 'catch shares,' is a management system that assigns "property values to various stakeholders, including individuals, communities, and cooperatives, with the goal of establishing incentives to promote long-term sustainability of fish stocks."

The Hamilton Report further explains: "Catch shares are a family of policies… that can be customized to the particular circumstances of a community. All catch shares enable fishery management councils to establish the total amount of fish that can be caught based on sustainability criteria. But catch shares differ in their implementation. One version…assigns tradeable fishing rights to individuals, giving each fisherman a share of the total allowable catch. This design aims to encourage fishermen with low costs to purchase shares from those with high costs, improving catch efficiency while compensating those who choose to sell their shares. Another type of catch shares allows a group of fishermen to cooperate on harvest strategies, co-management, and marketing. And yet another type gives a fishing community an exclusive privilege to harvest a designated area of the ocean." Despite criticism, objection to consolidation, a bias against smaller operators, and the decline in related new boat construction, roughly half of the fish caught in the US is harvested from a fishery under catch share management.

All this, nonetheless, does not address the resultant threat to the economic stability of the industry. Is there anything to be done?

Well, yes, there might be another way to "invent" additional value to the given catch in whatever amount by using every fish, and every part of those fish, as a new contribution to the total revenue.

According to *Wasted Catch*, an excellent study by Oceana, "global by-catch may amount to 40 percent of the world's catch, totaling 63 billion pounds per year. Some fisheries discard more fish at sea than what they bring to port, in addition to injuring and killing thousands of whales, dolphins, seals, sea turtles and sharks each year. While by-catch data is often outdated and incorrect, researchers estimate that 17-22 percent of US catch is discarded every year and…could amount to 2 billion pounds every year, equivalent to the entire annual catch of many other fishing nations around the world." So, there is one powerful step to be taken: find more value in the 20% of the fish already taken – as fertilizer or fish oil or fish feed – a market value now abandoned for lack of innovation or effort.

Further, the Iceland Ocean Cluster, a cooperative of start-up marine-based companies, has taken a second, even more imaginative step – the utilization of 100% of every fish taken – filets for traditional food processing, roes and milt for caviar and other food products, liver for canned goods and pate, fish oils and intestines for enzymes in skin creams, cosmetics, and medical products, livers for Omega-3 oil in capsules, skin transformed into leather for clothing, medical products, and collagen, and heads and bones dried and transformed into protein and supplements for export to Asian markets. All these revenues are new, measured in new employment and increased return from an existing product by creating demand for an existing resource. All this value is available to the industry now, without another fish taken.

PROTECTING OUR OCEAN

E.O. Wilson, the eminent scientist and ecologist, has suggested that in order to protect the world's natural resources against the challenges of climate change and other destructive phenomena – and to conserve these resources and allow the biosphere to recover and to sustain the needs of our future population growth – we should set aside some 50% of earth in reserves to meet that essential goal.

In the context of the ocean, this initiative has taken the form of Marine Protected Areas, called MPAs, in an international effort to identify and preserve from harmful practice some of the most fertile ocean places around the world. It is an ongoing effort providing a source of optimism and inspiration for ocean conservationists worldwide.

There are some 5,000 MPAs already designated, comprising approximately 2.65 million square kilometers, representing 0.8% of the world's 360 million square kilometers of ocean and 2% of the 147 million square kilometers of ocean under national jurisdiction. These areas are protected as marine parks, national monuments, and environmental reserves under the various legislative regimes of national or state governments. The largest areas are located in the Republic of Kiribati, Australia, the United States, the Northern Marianas Island, the Galapagos in Ecuador, and Columbia. Most MPAs, however, are small: ranging from 5 to 500 square kilometers, located mainly along the coasts, leaving a vast area of oceanic and deep-water habitats unprotected. The number continues to grow.

Joshua Reichert, Executive Vice President of the Pew Charitable Trust, who has overseen its environmental projects for more than 30 years, addresses the best way to restore and maintain ocean health as follows: "First, we need to curb overfishing. We must prevent the destruction of essential habitat needed by the ocean life by banning the most destructive fishing gear and practices, and by halting the decline of wetlands and other areas of critical importance to marine life. Also essential is to protect the world's oceans that are still relatively pristine. One of the most effective ways to accomplish this is by establishing marine reserves where no fishing and other extractive activities are allowed."

Not everyone agrees, and there remains opposition both within governments and by marine fishing and mining interests, that see such designations as infringement on commercial activity. There are also questions of definition, regulation, stewardship resources, and enforcement by smaller states with limited budgets and the most to lose. The Pew Trust joined with partners to initiate satellite surveillance of some of these protected areas, to track vessels fishing illegally therein, and some government have gone so far as to make arrests, to assess fines and penalties, and, in some cases, to destroy the offending vessels.

What is to be celebrated about the MPA movement is its focus on the most productive places where marine species – plant and animal – can find safety, resilience, and renewal. These places are incubators and sustainers of ocean biodiversity; they contain knowledge and potential for our future that we might not yet know or understand. They begin to encompass a logical collection of ecosystems, not just in the tropics, but in far northern and southern waters, in Antarctica and the Arctic, and along the coastal edge, where salt and fresh water systems meet, as part of the global cycle of sustaining water.

Many individuals and environmental organizations are working hard and long on this project. Among the many efforts that give us optimism and courage about the future of our natural world and our place within it, surely the collaboration and continuing designation of marine protected areas demonstrates a most collective and engaged success. Less than 1% of the ocean has been conserved to date – a far cry from E.O. Wilson's 50%. The benefit of every incremental step accrues to each one of us, advances the awareness and logic of our need to conserve ocean resources for family and community, and argues for national and international commitment to such behavior for the protection of us all.

HOPEFUL NUMBERS

I was heartened by a report from the Yale Program on Climate Change Communications, the result of an annual survey taken in the United States measuring the state of public awareness and political views on issues relating to climate reality, global warming, political bias, and the implication of measured opinion for the future.

Surveying results from 2008 though 2018, the Yale report notes a significant shift upward from 5 to 9% by registered voters in terms of understanding and concern over the existence and human cause of climate change, registered voters who are "somewhat" or "very" worried about global warming and the need to take reactive measures. While the increases vary according to political party orientation, the numbers in support are at an all-time high.

The survey also addresses four different types of proposed national policies to reduce carbon pollution, decrease dependence on fossil fuels, and promote clean energy. Specifically, it sought opinion on 1) The Green New Deal, a ten-year plan to invest in green technology, energy efficiency, and infrastructure to make the nation 100% reliant on clean renewable resources; 2) The Clean Carbon Plan, the setting of strict carbon dioxide emission limits on coal-fired plants to reduce global warming and improve public health; 3) A Revenue-Neutral Carbon Tax, requiring fossil fuel companies to pay a carbon tax that would be directed to reduce other taxes, such as income, in equal amount; and 4) A Fee and Dividend Proposal, requiring fossil fuel companies to pay a fee on carbon pollution, the funds to be distributed as a dividend to US citizens in equal amounts.

These would seem controversial and unlikely, given the early results of the survey. But here are the results for the Green New Deal support: 81% positive for all registered voters; 92% of Democrats; 88% of Independents; and 64% of Republicans. Or, how about these results for Fee and Dividend? 63% of registered voters; 78% of Democrats; 66% of Independents; and 39% of Republicans.

Frankly, I found these numbers astonishing. Yes, you can quibble about methodology and all the rest when challenging the accuracy of such surveys, but consider the relative shift in favor of ideas that just a few years ago would have not even been considered by the public. I take great heart from this response. It signals a serious shift in awareness and understanding of the need for new values, structures, and behaviors if we are to meet the critical challenge of changing climate made more evident to us all.

Credit communications. Credit the press that has reported the climate-related consequences affecting people all over the world. Credit the scientists who have steadfastly promoted the data, the evidence, in the face of irrational denial. Credit the authors of a library of important books on the environment predicting the impacts to come, even if not then apparent to us all. Credit the few, dedicated politicians who have spoken constantly to the legislature and the leadership, even if persistently ignored. Credit the citizens themselves who have seen the evidence, taken stock, and intend to apply that understanding as political will.

REVOLUTION

Thousands of research studies performed by thousands of scientists provide evidence of human-generated activities that define the reality of climate change already despoiling our air, fresh water, land, and ocean.

Thousands of extreme weather events attributed to climate change – drought, storm, fire – desiccate our agricultural lands, inundate our coasts, burn our forests, and distribute the toxic consequences via the atmosphere and the sea. Thousands of lives are lost; thousands of communities are disrupted; thousands of jobs are destroyed; thousands and thousands and thousands of dollars of property value and financial resources are consumed by indifference and denial.

Thousands of organizations, communities, churches and professional associations have expressed their dissatisfaction with the lack of any meaningful political response to the accelerating evidence of dramatic negative consequences of climate change – across the world and at every level of society.

Thousands of news reports, editorials, legislative initiatives, alternative technologies, and innovative proposals have been put forward, only to be ridiculed and ignored.

Thousands of individuals have petitioned, voted, demonstrated, and volunteered, expressing their concern with this critical condition, their anger with this political irresponsibility, their demand that this problem be faced now and that necessary steps be urgently taken to address this challenge to future survival.

Thousands of thousands of thousands add up to millions and millions worldwide. Indeed, billions, as the fate of all of us – and our children – may be at stake.

To no avail.

The lack of care, concern, and courage by world leaders is reprehensible. Where are the climate candidates? Where are the crusading legislators? Where are the social consciences beyond those, elected to represent our best interest as a nation, who mock the evidence, protect the status quo, subvert any meaningful response, and sabotage even the idea of change? And, worst of all, where is the opposition to those who, beyond denial, act overtly to capitalize personally or corporately at our expense?

Where is the outrage?

The usual tools for communication seem not to serve. Thousands of letters and calls to legislators do not convert to political results. Thousands of individuals engaged in specific social media campaigns are ignored. Thousands of people in the streets hardly make the nightly news. Thousands of strangers affected in faraway places seem of no significance. Thousands of urban victims of super storms – the flooded subways, inundated coastal businesses, and washed-out homes – are quickly forgotten.

What if we foment a viral revolution, an "electronic climate spring," where we concentrate all our rage in one place until we are heard? What if we combine all our thousands, even millions, of voices, in a "virtual square," where we actively and repeatedly demonstrate to the "leader of free world" our collective power, unite in a digital chant from the world over, bringing together every citizen of every country who believes that the United States, as a responsible nation, must meet the threat of climate change now with real, substantive, proactive policy and legislative action in every aspect of governance? What if we collect and concentrate all our discontent and aspiration in one revolutionary space, time and again, perhaps day after day, where the full length, breadth, and depth of our demand will be so strong, so loud, so incontrovertible, so constant, and so politically right that our will cannot be denied?

Here is the message: "As a Citizen of the Ocean, the United States, and the World, I demand your immediate national leadership, executive commitment, and uncompromised personal support for direct action at every level in every department of government to meet the worldwide challenge of climate change to every aspect of our lives."

What if thousands of us accept the challenge to respond? What if thousands and thousands of us repeat our message until the White House servers are full of our voices? What if we "occupy" the White House electronically with the reality of our anger and expectation? What if we engage the full network of climate-committed organizations and their collective members? What if we engage others from outside the United States who have their own legitimate interest in our political and economic leadership toward a climate solution? What if we use the collective audacity of millions to transcend the volume of deniers, the narrow-minded legislators, the captive representatives of vested interests, the paralyzed bureaucrats, and the fearful political advisors and speak directly to the President? Speak freely. Call him out. Make him respond. Make him do more than speak his mind through intermediaries and releases. Make him prove his personal understanding of the profound challenge we face in climate change. Make him respond to his constituents without equivocation. Make him turn his presidency into a constant exercise in global statesmanship that will make far more difference to the world than anything else on the modern political agenda. Our health depends on it. Our wealth depends on it. Our national security depends on it. Our moral standing in the world depends on it. Our future depends on it. Our survival as a civilization depends on it.

EIGHT URGENT STEPS FOR OUR OCEAN PLANET

The challenges facing the world ocean have never been more critical. Almost every aspect of the ocean – its health, its productivity, its management – is under attack, and, while there are thousands of organizations and millions of people engaged in response, we still seem to be losing ground (or, in this case, water).

How to choose among the issues and the strategies? What individual or organization makes the most sense as focused resistance? What specific action should be taken, at what level of living? As an individual, a family, a community, a nation? And how do we project the outcome, and by what measure? I ask these questions every day, and every day I can come up with a different conclusion about where to place my energy and resolve as a Citizen of the Ocean.

We like lists, as order and instruction. Here is one published in May, 2019, by a collective of 15 distinguished international ocean scientists and policy experts, under the coordination of the International Union for the Conservation of Nature, entitled *Eight Urgent, Fundamental and Simultaneous Steps Needed to Restore Ocean Health, and the Consequences for Humanity and the Planet of Inaction or Delay.* There are other such lists, but this one will serve to illustrate the need, the range, and the urgency of directed response.

The questions posed are as follows:

- What are the major gaps in ocean protection and conservation?
- Which three interventions would make the biggest positive impacts in arresting the trajectory of ocean decline?
- What one action should be taken within the next three years if we are going to make a difference in time, or, what do we have to do now because delay will mean the negative impacts will be irreversible and catastrophic?
- Are there recent trends in ocean change that, in your view, are cause for concern and need more attention?
- If you had the power, what would you change or implement tomorrow?

In its published report, the group consensus identified the following eight priority actions needed to divert ecological disaster in the global ocean:

- Address climate change and implement policies to limit temperature rise to 1.5 C, but to prepare for 2-3 C rise;
- Secure a robust and comprehensive High Seas Treaty with a Conference of the Parties and a Scientific Committee;
- Enforce existing standards for Marine Protected Areas, extending their scope to fully protect at least 30% of the ocean while ensuring effective management for 100% of the rest of the ocean;
- Adopt a precautionary pause on deep-sea mining to allow time to gain sufficient knowledge and understanding to support informed decisions and effective management;
- End overfishing and destructive practices including illegal, unreported and unregulated fishing;
- Radically reduce marine water pollution;
- Provide a financing mechanism for ocean management and protection;
- Scale up scientific research on the ocean and increase transparency and accessibility of ocean data from all sources.

The paper adds one important perspective not always included: "Once detrimental or negative changes have occurred, they may lock in place and may not be reversible. Each change may represent a loss to humanity of resources, ecosystem function, oxygen production and species. Thus, we may think we can simply stop doing things and assume that previous conditions…will return, when in reality the longer we pursue damaging actions, the more we close the path to recovery and better ocean health and greater benefits for humanity in the future."

The prospect described is daunting. Just pick one recommended action, and consider how much planning, effort, funding, and governance would be required to come close to meeting the transformative objective. The paper concludes, "The challenges may seem insurmountable, but if we act now, and enforce the eight themes outlined, even with our current state of knowledge…a more positive and sustainable future for the ocean is possible. Acting now with urgency and a massive increase in the level of ambition has to be the no-regrets policy to protect us and future generations from our short-termism and ignorance about why a healthy ocean should and does matter to all of us." Do we have the ambition to survive? Now, there's a question.

THE OCEAN COMMONS

Most of us are familiar, from our colonial history lessons, with the idea of the commons, that central portion of land, around which a settlement was built, shared by all for pasturage of animals, agriculture, and general well-being. We may also be aware of the influential essay, *Tragedy of the Commons*, by ecologist Garrett Hardin, first published in the journal *Science* in 1968, which describes a dilemma arising from a situation in which multiple individuals, acting independently and rationally consulting their own self-interest, will ultimately deplete a shared limited resource, even when it is clear that it is not in anyone's long-term interest for this to happen. Turning to the ocean, we realize that it is the greatest commons of them all.

International law delimits national interest in ocean resources to an "exclusive economic zone" up to 200 miles offshore. The balance – that is, 64% of the ocean surface and 90% of its volume – lies outside such governance and includes the high seas, the ocean floor and subsoil, an enormous compendium of natural resources to include all marine species, minerals, chemicals, and genetic resources of incalculable value to human kind.

It is a vast challenge to protect, manage, and sustain such a resource, especially when agreement involves multiple levels of governance and a broad spectrum of public and private enterprise. The tragedy of the ocean commons is evinced by the intrusion of polluting elements from the nations and their self-interests that invade and destroy the shared value without constraint and without question.

It may be the most important geopolitical question we face. How do we govern, how do we manage, the ocean outside national jurisdiction to use it responsibly, to sustain its value near and long-term, and to assure its potential forever for the benefit of all mankind?

We have many tools in place that have, and can continue, to address the issue aggressively: local management plans, marine protected areas, spatial planning, pilot zoning projects, environmental assessments, management training, and transfer of an ever-expanding reservoir of ocean information and technology. We also have many organizations – the United Nations General Assembly, the UN Intergovernmental Oceanographic Commission, the UN Food and Agriculture Organization, the UN International Maritime Organization, the International Seabed Authority, the Convention on Biological Diversity, the Conference on Sustainable Development, various fisheries agreements, the Antarctic treaties, the UN Law of the Sea, and many more – forming a skein of overlapping policy-making and regulatory structures that account for what progress has been made over the last few decades.

Some would argue that that progress has been very little. Serious problems do remain: data gaps, irregular process, limited coordination, inequitable geographic coverage, lack of time and financial resources, regulatory failures, legal limitations, outdated laws, and inadequate compliance and enforcement. But let's not rush to the cynical conclusion. The irony is that despite these inhibitions, we do have the knowledge, the principles, and organizations in place to be successful. If we could address these existing issues, invigorate these existing organizations, we could, by applying the tools already in hand, make a powerful difference in our ability to address the deteriorating condition of the ocean commons.

It seems complicated, and I fear the powers that be will opt for another noble declaration of principles or a new, larger, all-encompassing bureaucracy. What we need is willpower and action, not ideals and intentions. In the end, it must come down to agreement on what is our ultimate self-interest. Do we care enough? Do we understand the ocean's capacity to provide the nurturing imperatives for our future lives? Do we want to live in a world where everyone, not just a few, has access to the common wealth of the ocean for generations to come? Can it be that simple?

DESALINATION

The persistent drought in California in the United States is a visible realization of our lack of water awareness and its destructive undermining of the financial structure and social organization we have built in that most progressive state, in that most successful global economy. If we fail in California, how can we succeed anywhere else? How can we avoid the coming collapse of world water?

At the most reductive level, the traditional water supply system in California has been overwhelmed by climate, industrial agriculture, and water-rich consumption that has been the envy of the world but can survive no longer without revolutionary change. If there is not enough water on the mountaintops to feed the watersheds, rivers, and reservoirs, then where will the requisite water come from?

In 2012, the San Diego County Water Authority signed an agreement to build the largest desalination plant in the United States. The process is not new; it is applied today in some 21,000 desalination plants in over 120 countries, including Italy, Australia, Spain, Greece, Portugal, Japan, China, India, United Arab Emirates, Malta, Cape Verde, and Cyprus, producing more than 3.5 billion gallons of potable water per day. Saudi Arabia leads the world, meeting 70% of the daily needs of its population.

The San Diego project was proposed to begin in 2015 and to provide 7% of the Authority's demand by 2020. The plant is to be built and operated by Poseidon Water, a private investor-owned company that develops water and wastewater infrastructure. The contract is for 30 years, after which the Authority can purchase the plant for $1. The company is also building a 10-mile pipeline to deliver treated water inland to the Authority's aqueduct system where it can augment existing collected or natural supply to serve the needs of the 24 regional member water agencies serving 3.1 million people.

The plant occupies 6 acres of the 388-acre ocean-front site of the Encina Power Station that for 50 years has run on oil and natural gas, releasing emissions, and requiring a large dredged lagoon to hold sea water for cooling and to receive plant effluent – a stagnant, stinking reminder of an old technology. The adjacent desalination plant will use a reverse osmosis process with its source water coming from the generating plant cooling supply, treated and pumped under pressure through membranes to remove salt and other microscopic impurities.

In the past, the primary objections to desalination have been salt residue, corrosion, habitat destruction, and cost. The Poseidon plant has undergone comprehensive review by the local, state, and federal agencies determined to protect its constituents and the environment. For every two gallons treated, one will be quality drinking water and the other diluted salt content for return to the ocean. The plant will run on Encina electricity to power high-speed pumps at market rates built into the contract. The approvals indicate that there will be no noise, no odor, and no environmental impact. Remarkably, the surrounding land has already been renewed by the prospect of the new plant and has been re-developed by the Authority to transform the embayment into a viable environment for marine life and community activities.

The San Diego region has been a center for the development of international desalination technology. The reverse osmosis process was born from a local company in the 1960s. There are some 35 related companies in the area employing 2,200 people and generating over $200 million in annual revenue. According to the Authority, the Poseidon Project "will have significant economic benefit for the region, including $350 million in spending during construction, 2,400 construction-related jobs, and $50 million in annual spending throughout the region once the desalination plant is operational. For the region, the facility will create jobs, generate tax revenue, improve water quality and enhance water reliability with a new drought-proof supply."

Drought-proof?

These hopeful numbers and language are the typical political arguments that have been used to justify new technology for a long time. The financial estimates may or may not be predictable or accurate, but the ultimate return is inevitable when there is suddenly no more water available, we need the salt water turned fresh, and the cost is priceless.

OCEAN ALCHEMY

In the middle ages, as science emerged from religion, there came a number of visionary inventors who organized a worldview that came to incorporate the discoveries of the time: the movement of the planets and stars, elements of a natural physical system, a new order of things, and inter-connections and changes that extended knowledge beyond superstition to theories of man and the universe. Using this awareness, expressed in a laboratory, alchemists became so bold as to think they could turn base metal into gold. In a sense, that endeavor represents the origin of modern process and invention that has led us to transformative technologies such as nuclear fusion and fission, genetic modification, and artificial intelligence. How do we change one thing into another, the value measured as exponential benefit for all mankind?

A contemporary example: in Kiunga, Kenya – a small fishing village on the Indian Ocean, population 3500 – a non-governmental organization, Give Power, inaugurated the first solar-powered water farm in Africa. It turns seawater into clean and sustainable drinking water, using a filtration system that turns brackish salt water into enough drinking water for up to 35,000 people every day – ten times the need.

No part of the world is immune to the pollution, over-consumption, and commodification of water from land sources for irrigation, sanitation, and manufacturing, exhaustion of the most valuable natural element on earth, without which none of us can survive. I have written and argued elsewhere for a "water ethic," an acknowledgment that present rates of consumption and corruption of hydraulic systems cannot be prolonged, a fact exacerbated by climate conditions, increased drought, failed ground water re-capture and reserve, and the collapse of aquifers. The water crisis in upon us, evident in cities and rural areas, in the north and south, and everywhere in between where supply so evidently exceeds demand and people suffer by deprivation and death. The equation is direct and simple, and the consequences are real. No one is immune.

According to the World Health Organization, 844 million people around the globe lack access to clean drinking water, and hundreds of thousands are dying from waterborne diseases. The numbers are staggering: some 2 billion people live in water-scarce areas, a number estimated to rise to 3.5 billion by 2025. When you turn on the tap and let it run, take that long shower, whoever you are, wherever you are, the effect is the same: depletion of a finite supply of freshwater that does not bode well for the future. It cannot go on forever.

Some obvious solutions: first; mandatory conservation, re-construction of unmaintained and inefficient treatment and distribution systems, and re-organization of industrial water processes around regulatory standards for re-use and sustainability. Second; desalination of ocean water as the only alternative means to compensate for the landside loss. Desalination has long been argued against as unnecessary, energy expensive, and environmentally polluting – arguments informed and accepted with a false sense of security. But all those arguments go quickly away when the harsh reality of depletion is revealed; the rivers and the taps run dry, disease increases, economies fail, chaos ensues. This may sound melodramatic, but it is not. Think about those 3.5 billion people with no water.

Desalination of ocean water meets this need on the required scale. Historically, 'desal' plants in the United States have been opposed by financiers, municipal leaders, and even environmentalists as too costly and unnecessary; only a few have been built, but that will surely change when faced with no alternative. All the conventional economics and politics will be contradicted; there will be no other choice. To predict the future with any responsible vision, take a look at Kiunga: the small, inexpensive, transportable system fired by the sun has made an immediate difference between life and death, not just for the 3,500 locals, but for the 31,500 more for whom that water will be accessible. Let us then embrace this ocean alchemy – new gold, as fresh water transmuted from the sea.

SUSTAINABILITY

Sustainability is the word we hear most often in discussions of how to deal progressively with the social and economic challenges resulting from the world's radical population growth, global economy, and voracious appetite for non-renewable natural resources to meet those needs over time. The most common usage derives from the 1987 United Nations Brutland Commission Report that defined sustainable development as that "which meets the needs of the present without compromising the ability of future generations to meet their own needs." From this has emerged an industry of academic proposals, new standards and accreditations, non-governmental organizations and policy institutions devoted to the amplification of the concept, in the form of environmental management, financial analyses and planning processes. The alleviation of poverty, social justice, human rights, and cultural traditions are essential to the response. In some cases, sustainability is measured and analyzed; expressed by a formula relating population, affluence and technology as measurable elements of an equation; to a newly inclusive accounting system; or to a calculation of previously ignored factors reduced to an index. In others, sustainability seems like an idealistic, unobtainable philosophical concept that offers hope, however illusionary and elusive.

Sustainability, as it relates to the ocean, may seem to exceed efforts beyond the obvious applications regarding regenerative fisheries and sustainable seafood, including: species protection, regional quotas, gear restrictions, and regulated market forces, aquaculture; a means to increase alternative supply against insatiable demand; coastal management and marine protected areas; schemes to protect inshore artisanal fishing, coral reefs, seed ground, and sheltering habitat against extreme weather, sea level rise, and the predations of resort and high rise developers.

But if you step back, and take the broadest ecosystem view, the ocean becomes an enormous contributor to any new strategy of resilience, maintenance, and enhancement of global bio-diversity and capacity, essential to the life-support system of the earth. As we continue to deplete underground aquifers, to increase irrigated land, to disrupt and pollute streams and rivers, the ocean becomes even more valuable as a primary component of the world water cycle – a necessary circulation, filtration, and purification system, and an inevitable source of desalinated drinking water to meet future global demand. As the ocean is essential to our need for fresh water, as water security and food security are linked, as food security and the alleviation of poverty are linked, and as alleviation of poverty is key to civilization, justice and peace, the ocean simply cannot go the way of the earth, be brutalized, ignored, taken for granted, or abandoned.

The ocean is the true commons; a vast reservoir of natural capital, without which the mechanics of the earth will break down. There is much talk of a "green" economy: a shift away from relentless growth fueled by forests, minerals, and fossil fuels – resources stolen from the past and the future – toward renewable energy, pricing that incorporates the true value of ecosystem service, and development based not on consumption but rather on utility and quality of life. All those new ideas for changed behavior on land are welcome and must be supported. However, the green economy will not succeed without the blue economy, which includes in the calculation the ocean as a redeeming source of renewable protein, energy, fresh water, and biodiversity with unimagined implication for the future of human survival.

The blue economy has a chance to succeed because it is open and free. No one owns it; no one can fence it; no one can master it, no matter how hard they try. Oh, to be sure, governments will continue to assert their exclusive economic rights along their coasts, corporations will still seek to impose their extraction values offshore, but it will not be enough; it will only postpone the inevitable and prolong the decline. When we learn to see the ocean as integral to the land – when we design physical places, make financial and social decisions, and take political action based on that symbiosis – then, we may well have achieved the means by which to build a world that is truly sustainable.

COASTAL STRATEGIES AND INVENTION
Facing the prospect of climate change, we appear to have three choices: do nothing, change our lives through the exercise of restraint, or change our lives more dramatically in response to environmental and economic challenges. We see these scenarios acted out daily: on the talk shows and blogs, in the press, and in halls of governance. Those that deny or belittle the scientific evidence or have other, clearly

vested interests in the status quo, continue to confuse the debate. Legislation is compromised, diluted, or stalled.

If we look at sea level rise and increasing storm activity and surge as functions of climate change, it is clear that something must be done in the coastal zone to protect life, property, and natural resources.

In 1998, NOAA summarized our coastal responses as follows:

(1) Accommodate. Under this approach, vulnerable areas continue to be occupied, accepting the greater degree of effects, such as flooding, saltwater intrusion, and erosion; advanced coastal management is used to avoid the worst impacts; improved early warning systems alert inhabitants of catastrophic events; and building codes are modified to strengthen the most vulnerable structures.

(2) Protect. Under this approach, population centers, high-value economic activities, and critical natural resources, are defended by sea walls, bulkheads, saltwater intrusion barriers; other infrastructure investments are made; and "soft" structural options such as periodic beach re-nourishment, landfill, dune maintenance or restoration, and wetlands creation are carried out.

(3) Retreat. Under this approach, existing structures and infrastructure in vulnerable areas are abandoned, inhabitants are resettled, government insurance subsidies are withdrawn, and new development is required to be set back specific distances from the shore, as appropriate.

What is most revealing about these recommendations is that they offer nothing new by way of systems or values, planning, or financial incentives for alternative development or management. Indeed, retreat may be the only option if, as, recently, in Bangladesh, an entire region was inundated with complete destruction of a delta area and massive loss of life.

What might be added to the NOAA summary is a fourth response:

4) Invent. Reorganize governance boundaries into regional organizations, apply planning concepts that align development with the natural protection features of the environment, provide economic incentives for alternative, survivable residential design and construction, nurture ocean-related industry while locating non-waterfront dependent business in safer locales, remove exclusive ownership from the coast area and open beaches and natural areas to public for active and passive recreation.

These are just a few ideas – some radical, some inevitable. We risk much if we do nothing, nor can we expect real change to come through incremental restraint. We can, however, opt for invention; for the application of our imagination and energy, of our science and technology, and of new understanding of the value of natural systems as constructive contributors to the betterment of our lives, rather than destructive forces beyond our control and challenging our survival.

THE POLAR CODE
According to its mission statement, the International Maritime Organization is "a specialized agency of the United Nations and the global standard-setting authority for the safety, security and environmental performance of international shipping. Its main role is to create a regulatory framework for the shipping industry that is fair and effective, universally adopted and universally implemented."

The statement continues: "Shipping is a truly international industry, and it can only operate effectively if the regulations and standards are themselves agreed, adopted and implemented on an international basis. And IMO is the forum at which this process takes place."

 "IMO measures cover all aspects of international shipping – including ship design, construction, equipment, manning, operation and disposal – to ensure that this vital sector ... remains safe, environmentally sound, energy efficient and secure."

When faced with any management challenge, it is a good thing to define goals and objectives, organize and clarify procedures, and begin to design the specific steps to be taken – anticipating the questions, providing the answers, and putting forward the regulations and reviews for implementation of response. We complain of such structures, as they are typically embodied in vast, often faceless, bureaucracies, dense manuals of requirements, rules for inspections and evaluations, additions and revisions, often seemingly tyrannical, even, when realized and justified for the public good. When we think of "Brussels" or "the Beltway" we think of such agencies and sometimes recoil.

But, in fact, such responses are the inevitable complicated and specifically detailed requirements necessary to deal with equally complicated and specifically detailed circumstances. Let me give you one example: the IMO text for a new Polar Code to govern all aspects of shipping in the Arctic and Antarctic regions, an area rapidly changing as a result of melting sea-ice and the potential opening for polar waters to maritime exploitation and endeavor. The purpose of the Code "is to provide for safe ship operation and the protection of the polar environment by addressing risks present in polar waters and not adequately mitigated by other instruments of the Organization."

It is an astonishing document. The contents include Polar Water Operational Manual, Ship Structure, Subdivision and Stability, Watertight and Weather tight Integrity, Machinery Installations, Fire Safety and Protection, Life-Saving Appliances and Arrangement, Safety of Navigation, Communication, Voyage Planning, Manning and Training, Prevention of Pollution by Oil, Control of Pollution by Noxious Liquids in Bulk, Prevention of Pollution by Harmful Substances Carried by Sea in Packaged Form, Prevention of Pollution by Sewage from Ships, Prevention of Pollution by Garbage from Ships, and various sections and appendices providing additional guidance for the implementation of these standards and requirements. Each chapter is detailed down to minute specifications, planning documents, inspections, and licensing enforcement.

In a Preamble, the Code acknowledges various limitations: for example, "that the polar waters impose additional navigational demands beyond those normally encountered…in many areas chart coverage may not currently be adequate for coastal navigation" or "that coastal communities in the Arctic could be…vulnerable to human activities, such as ship operation." In effect, the document addresses the most basic technical engineering standards to diminish risk of accident from ship operation in an uncharted and vulnerable region, but requires no capacity for rescue or environmental response to error, accident, or disaster. I cannot argue with the purpose of the Code, its thoroughness, or specific recommendations (down to pocket knives and extra batteries in the survival kits); it is all good, prescient, and actuarially responsible, albeit theoretical, in advance of potential increased ship operations in polar waters.

But, it seems to me, fundamentally lacking, by not also requiring the operational preparedness demanded by the possible failure of the Code to anticipate all risk taken by ships in these waters at all. Should we really allow vessels passage into water that has no comprehensive navigational aid based on fully surveyed channels? Should we allow such passages with no equally detailed system for emergency response? Should we allow for any risk of pollution by oil, sewage, or other noxious substances with no established capacity or plan in place for immediate reaction, access to an accident site, systematic cleanup material pre-placed, mitigation technology available and appropriate to severe polar conditions, assignment and acceptance of responsibility clearly stated, adequate and comprehensive insurance, environmental protection bond or other financial guarantees secured, defined legal obligations of ship operators, and judicial procedures and jurisdictions established to adjudicate the inevitable liability disputes?

Should not these questions be asked and answered before a single ship, meeting the Polar Code or otherwise, operates in polar waters? Is the IMO the agency for such deliberation? If not, who is?

ARCTIC FISHERIES MANAGEMENT

As fisheries worldwide are being seriously depleted by over-fishing and illegal, unregulated harvest in the ocean beyond the interests and protections of national exclusive economic zones, focus has shifted from artisanal and coastal fishing to new grounds in faraway places, accessible by larger vessels and new technologies and, presumably, filled with all those fish that had previously escaped the innumerable hooks and insatiable nets. With the melting of sea ice in the Arctic and Antarctic, those areas have been inevitably invaded, raising obvious concerns that the ethos of total consumption will extend to those areas, with depletion and collapse a foreseeable outcome. The pressure is enormous, and 'fisheries' has joined the major categories for natural resource exploitation in those regions – oil, gas, precious metals, and now protein suddenly available in these remote waters.

If we look to the Arctic as the most viable example, and as the area grows annually with faster and more extensive melting of the sea ice, the temptation to exploit grows exponentially. What to do?

In July 2015, five peripheral nations met in Oslo, Norway, to discuss regulatory prospects. In a joint declaration, they recognized the removal of barriers to the area as a result of climate change, the threat to a unique, shared ecosystem, the environmental dangers, the problems of jurisdiction, the lack of scientific knowledge, and the threat by commercial interests with no management regulations or authority in place. They also acknowledged the value of the traditional knowledge and experience, and the impact of new development on these local users and their communities.

The self-imposed limits were conservative: no authorized presence of national vessels outside one or more regional fisheries management organizations; establishment of a joint program of scientific research; compliance of interim measures with relevant international law; coordination of monitoring control and surveillance activities in the area; assurance that non-commercial fishing does not undermine the agreement; and commitment to respect, cooperation, and continuing process.

In April 2017, according to a report by the Pew Charitable Trusts, these five nations, joined by delegations from Iceland, China, the European Union, Japan, and South Korea, joined forces in a legally binding agreement that would prevent commercial fishing in 1.1 million square miles of the Central Arctic Ocean until a science-based fishery management measure is in place. The new proposal built on and extended the earlier precautionary approach by specifying a joint research program, formally incorporating indigenous knowledge into management policies, and completing the legal description of the area to be covered, procedures for decision-making, and outlining the conditions for additional management and oversight. This resolve was far more direct, proscriptive, and responsive to the sudden increase by 40% of the area in region – ice-free as open water – for the first time in human history.

I never know quite what to make of these declarations. On paper, on the surface, they communicate real intent and purpose. But I never know what happens after: how the research projects are implemented, researched, and published; how the regulatory specifics are defined, applied, and enforced; how the funds are accrued and distributed; whether what is said is what is meant, whether what is meant is what is done, whether what is done actually relates to and advances the proposal. I tend to be disappointed when, a year or so later, the follow-up meeting reveals some few incremental steps forward, much stasis, some unexpected circumstance that compromises or diverts from forward motion.

Diplomats, delegates, and negotiators survive by taking the longer view. They understand the inherent stop-time of consensus building. They see progress in terms of interval from report to report, conference to conference, declaration to declaration, election to election, over a temporary appointment or long career. They are accountable to best intentions, possible goals, shifting priorities, and rationalized outcomes. I often wonder what would be progress, to what ends, if the only participants at the table were the persons who actually lived in this changing circumpolar world: whose ideas, in short term reality, even as they are derived from the longest traditional view, would shape a very different message for all the world to hear.

WASTE-FREE OCEAN

Of all the waste deposited in the ocean, perhaps the best known is the plastic debris that shows up on our beaches, in the stomachs of fish and shore birds, in the enormous floating "island" of plastic in the Pacific Ocean, assembled there by the confluence of currents, preposterous in its scale, capturing the attention of international media. The situation is further exacerbated by the disintegration of plastic waste into microscopic particles that descend in the water column to intrude into the metabolism of marine species, with serious implications for reproduction and survival. Plastic is not the only waste entering the marine ecosystem; human waste, toxic manufacturing by-products, run-off of agricultural fertilizers and pesticide, radioactive material, oil and gas spills, and acid – all poisons resulting from the global mass consumption of carbon fuels add to what is the exponentially increasing decline of the ocean's capacity for future productivity, sustainability, and support for human survival.

The story is not new, and it is getting worse every day. What do we do about it?

We have seen the potential of recycling our waste. Glass bottles, aluminum cans, and certain scrap metals have found an industrial-scale technology and financial return, recovering and transforming these discarded products into new ones. Over 70% of newspapers and fiberboard, for example, are recycled and reformed into practical utility and new product.

But not plastic. In 2008, of the 33.6 million tons of post-consumer plastic waste in the United States, less than 15% was recycled or burned for energy. The balance was discarded into streams and rivers, and eventually into the ocean, or was buried in landfills where it will take centuries to decompose, leach chemicals and dyes into the groundwater, require some kind of expensive future remediation, and otherwise add insult to injury – and be removed from the "circular" economy that recycling represents.

This is tragic waste of waste. Some 4% of oil consumed annually in the world is used to manufacture plastic, an annual expenditure of resources and energy that ignores the residual value of what has already been expended. As importantly, that volume is withheld from the myriad alternative re-uses identified – thread, yarn, and fiber for clothing and durable products, injection-molded packaging for meat and vegetables, floor coverings, traffic cones, strapping tape, hoses, trash receptacles, truck cargo liners, clothes hangers, park benches, flower pots and seedling containers, stapler bodies, toys, foam peanuts, composite railroad ties, and aggregates for road surfaces, curbs, and building construction – these things, and many more, otherwise having to be made from new plastic with additional cost.

Because not all plastics are the same, there are different technologies required with varying operational and energy costs. This accounts for the very complicated identification codes found on plastic packaging, signaling the specific sorting required for recycling processes, a differentiation that complicates distribution and transportation, decreases the economic efficiency of any given treatment, and dissuades governments and individuals from investing the time and effort into maximizing the recycling movement. The resultant, less-than-profitable cost-benefit has been a disincentive to adequate investment, particularly in the US and in less affluent developing nations, and so, the plastic accumulates worldwide and the problem compounds itself globally.

Gold, silver, copper, and other precious metals can be recovered from e-waste – the enormous numbers of discarded cell phones, tablets, televisions and computers, other electronic devices, medical instruments, junked cars – in a form of urban mining that recycles these limited resources and obviates the need for new mining operations, particularly coastwise or in the deep ocean, where other unique marine resources are coincidentally destroyed by a crude, expensive, and unnecessary process.

Plastic recycling should be the same. Even though the unit pricing is radically different (an ounce of gold versus a ton of plastic), the exponential volume and ubiquitous need argues for scaled financial investment and favorable comparable returns. Some government incentives have been created, and some innovative companies have attempted to exemplify the process with success. MBA Polymers, an American company with processing plants in China, Austria, the United Kingdom, and the US, won the prestigious 2013 Katerva Award for "accelerating innovation for a sustainable future," by transforming such plastics into a pellet form for use in new products, expending less energy, conserving limited oil supplies, reducing carbon emissions, and reducing the landfill problem by keeping the plastic in circulation within the production system. Their inability to raise adequate capital for expansion of this endeavor in the US is a sad function of consumption-based conventional thinking, false calculation of corresponding value, and fragmented public concern.

There is hope, however. In Europe, The Waste-Free Ocean Foundation is dedicated to clean-up of marine litter. In the United States we see local communities expanding their recycling efforts; municipalities, even states, prohibiting plastic bags; and grassroots organization boycotting of wasteful practice and advocating for new behaviors. Is it possible that through such demands and changes, we might discover that there is enough plastic already extant in this world to meet our needs, and then some? Can we stop just throwing that plastic away? Can we convert that coastal trash and plastic island in the Pacific from a problem to a solution? Can we imagine and sustain a waste-free ocean?

BLUE ENERGY

Never have we needed alternative energy more than we do today. It has become finally clear that the harvest and burning of fossil fuels has caused massive damage to land, air, sea and global health, and that continued reliance on the cause to meet the crisis of the effect is suicidal. The financial markets, major investors, some governments, some of the big energy companies, and even some of the producing nations almost totally reliant on oil revenues, have realized that the fossil fuel era, for all its positives, is now over, done, and we need get on to our future.

The ocean will play an enormous part. We know the value of offshore wind, and finally, despite opposition by industry and some environmentalists, wind energy will be a significant source for power. Scandinavian and other European countries are well advanced. In the US, permit applications for offshore wind in the areas of five north Atlantic states – New York, Connecticut, Rhode Island, Massachusetts, and New Hampshire – exceed in projected production volume the generation of more than 20 modern nuclear plants. In Maine, the potential exceeds the total of those five states combined. After vested interest and political opposition, Maine's new governor has raised offshore wind generation to a primary premise on which the state's future is to be based.

There are also other technologies – hydropower well established, various projects for wave energy, tidal, and current generation underway, and renewed interest in geothermal energy linked to coast-based desalination plants. Finally, it seems that what were outlier, even radical, suggestions over time, now approach conventional wisdom. All good.

But not yet good enough. We are going to need further invention, capital investment, and new application of energy technology to augment, even replace, and render those methods described as interim. One such is based on salinity gradient power, the concept of energy generated by exchange of ions between freshwater and saltwater through membranes, with resultant heat or pressure build-up applied to drive turbines for electricity generation. Tim Smedley, a British journalist who writes most interestingly about climate issues and solutions, describes projects for this technology previously constructed in Sicily and Norway; both lapsed as difficult to scale and cost ineffective. But the Norwegian prototype has been revived, as a new pilot in Denmark, using much more efficient membranes, with an upscale potential of 1 Megawatt generation by 2022 – and a project similar to Sicily's has opened in the Netherlands at the Afsluitdijk dam, with freshwater on one side, saltwater on the other, now generating up to 50 KW of power. Smedley cites a study by Wageningen University in the Netherlands, identifying some 123 rivers worldwide that "have the technical potential for blue energy power generation exceeding 1 Gig watt to include the Zaire, Orinoco, Ganges, Niles, Mississippi, St. Lawrence, Parana, Zambezi, and Mekong." The coast as locus for innovation. The power edge.

An article published by the Electrochemical Society also discusses the further potential of blue energy, what it calls "osmotic power," a process that, if harnessed, Dr. Andrew Herring of the Colorado School of Mines, a Society advisor, describes as "free energy." As an example of such innovation, the Society also cites the work of Taek Dong Chung, a professor at the Korean National University in Seoul, who envisions the technology applied to salt-water powered computers, accelerated patch-based drug delivery, and water-splitting applications, the salt-water gradient powering semi-conductors to separate hydrogen and oxygen as a new source of energy transfer and delivery. The Society article concludes: "Blue Energy is just the tip of the iceberg when it comes to the energy/water nexus. In other areas of the field, researchers are working on developing membranes for more efficient water treatment, creating electrochemical devices to recycle dangerous fertilizer run-off to prevent algae blooms, processing urine to produce clean water with hydrogen as a by-product, and much more."

There you have it: the ocean, from wind to waste, serving our future.

DOWNSTREAM

We are all familiar with the threat of peak oil, that point in time when all the known oil reserves are exhausted and our reliance on that fossil fuel comes to an end. But what about peak water? A review of global fresh water reserves points to only four nations with large surplus: Canada, Russia, India and China.

The latter two come as a surprise: they are not due to vast concentrations of fresh water in the ice cap, but by the Greater Himalayas and Tibetan Plateau, that vast complex of mountains and glaciers that accounts for enormous annual run-off and long-term capture. Writing in an op-ed in the New York Times, Orville Schell provides the explanation. "Because the Tibetan Plateau and its environs shelter the largest perennial ice mass on the planet after the Arctic and Antarctica, it has come to be known as 'the Third Pole.' Its snowfields and glaciers feed almost every major river system of Asia during hot, dry seasons when the monsoons cease, and their melt waters supply rivers from the Indus in the west to the Yellow in the east, with the Ganges, Brahmaputra, Irrawaddy, Salween, Mekong and Yangtze Rivers in between." As an example, Schell cites the 1.7 mile Baishui Glacier situated near Lijiang, a town in southwest China, where the ice has receded 830 feet over two decades and respected glaciologists are predicting, if present conditions persist, the disappearance of two-thirds of the Plateau's ice by 2040, with the obvious ensuing consequence downstream.

When I am asked to define the limits of the ocean, I respond, "from the mountaintop to the abyssal plain." The ocean begins on Everest, and ends in the Marianas Trench, a transfer with all civilization in between. Some two billion people, for example, live downstream from Baishui and rely on the descending water network to hydrate themselves, their crops, their livestock, their industry, their leisure, and their spiritual lives. What happens along the way is not pretty. The water is wasted, mixed with sewerage and chemicals, diverted in massive irrigation schemes, and sold to vested interests to the extent that, in many rivers of the world, the outflow is exhausted and corrupted when it finally reaches its ultimate destination: the world ocean, where it is expected to be filtered and cleansed, circulated and evaporated, until it recycles in weather systems to be deposited by rain and snow again on the mountaintop.

But, as we know from evermore disturbing research, this natural ocean system is being challenged, if not overwhelmed, by the man-made conditions it is meant to correct. The pollutants are too strong, too many, too persistent, and, in certain instances, the natural circulation simply amplifies and distributes the toxic impact, recycling the negative and compromising the ocean's capacity for the positive.

The point is: as the polar regions are threatened, so, too, are the mountains and glaciers, the 'third pole,' about which not much thought is given, as least in the context of ocean conservation and sustainability. What we have here is yet another example of the intricate connections inherent in natural hydraulic systems, and of our indifference to, and misunderstanding of, how these systems work, thereby enabling consequences we cannot control. When you leave no trace in the mountains, then you have no resultant impact on the oceans. When factories and sewerage plants outflow clean water, they do not poison the fish or beaches along the coast. When fertilizer is organic and natural, it does not pollute wetlands or kill coral reefs. When we take only what we need upstream, then we permit the similar needs of our neighbors downstream to be met. When we modify our behavior on land, we make, there and then, a direct and equally conscious impact on the sea.

TRUST THE CHILDREN

I saw a comment on a social media page that asked when "the next generation" was going to step up and take responsibility for solutions to the world climate crisis. The question omitted the fact that the present generation had created the problem, and was prepared to leave the solution as a legacy to the next. Such a deal!

What is clear in the exponential evidence of the crisis – the wildfires, deforested watersheds, poisoned waterways, dead ocean zones, and so much more – affects all of us. Segmented responsibility is not the answer. What is certain is that all generations must engage, everywhere, and at every level of society. Governments must mobilize in response to the reality of cause and effect; communities, large or small, coastal or inland, must organize to protect and plan for what is already upon them; individuals of all ages must come together to mitigate the obvious and invent the structures and behaviors that will enable this requisite change and strategy for survival.

We are all frustrated by climate angst – the pervasive reveal of the consequence of what we have done to land and sea. When climate change is denied, I wonder: what is the underlying explanation? Vested interest? Fear of change? Indifference to destructive impact on others, elsewhere, even if that same destruction lurks just around the corner? It is, at once, explicable and illogical – a contradiction that enables the status quo and ignores the problem.

The commentator, of course, was uninformed. There are many, many examples worldwide where the next generation is committed and successful in raising awareness, demanding political action, and fomenting innovation and response. Our Children's Trust, an organization in Oregon in the United States, is challenging government for its failure to adhere to a legal obligation to protect Nature, a fundamental constitutional principle. When Children's Trust began, filing a first case in a local court, all the plaintiffs were under 18 years of age; they have persevered though the complex levels of the American justice system, winning decisions and appeals along the way.

Climate change is also becoming part of educational systems around the world. Italy requires "climate studies" as part of its national curriculum. "Ocean Literacy" standards, the inter-relation of the ocean to all disciplines, science and humanities, is being introduced in Europe and the United States, as an educational construct for progressive teaching and learning. From Scandinavia to Asia, the reality of climate change and the search for solutions is a phenomenon that can be measured in lesson plans, field trips, research projects, choices for higher education and careers, and even student walk-outs and strikes, condoned by teachers, to participate in protests in support of climate treaties and obligations and goals for sustainable development worldwide. If you march in the parades and attend the rallies, you will see how many of the participants are young adults and children fully committed to the agenda for change.

And there is the fascinating 16-year-old Swedish student who stood along on Friday afternoons before her national parliament to advocate for climate policy and launched, so astonishingly, an international coalition of young and old, and articulated a persistent, simple, and purposeful message that has galvanized the world through her personality, her clarity, and her success as an advocate in the global press, in myriad public events and conferences, and before the United Nations. Greta Thunberg, a young citizen of the world, was nominated for the Nobel Prize for Peace. She is a pure distillation of the next generation: wise, determined, and empowered. Call Greta and her young allies "children" at your peril. They are as mature as anyone who will study a problem, invent solutions, and commit to whatever it takes to build a better future for everyone.

To come to New York to address the UN, Greta chose to make a 3,500-mile, 15-day Atlantic crossing aboard a 60-foot sailboat; minimal carbon footprint, and instead of a corporate logo, "Listen to the Science" was the message on the sail. She described her ocean passage: "…it was just amazing to be in this wilderness and to see the wildlife there, with so many dolphins and other wildlife. And if it was calm, then during the nights you could see the stars…"

In her UN General Assembly address, she said: "We have not come here to beg the world leaders to care for our future. They have ignored us in the past, and they will ignore us again. We have come here to let them know that change is coming, whether they like it or not. The people will rise to the challenge. And since our leaders are behaving like children, we will have to take the responsibility they should have taken long ago." Who do we trust? Trust the children.

RECIPROCITY

When considering how we must deal with the myriad challenges to the world ocean, the conversation comes always to questions of behavior and values. What must change is how we interact with ocean systems, with the marine environment, with exploitation of marine resources, with coastal protection and development, and with the economic and social necessities we expect the ocean to provide. Given the immensity of the challenge, and the impossibility of a single solution, what specific interim steps must we take to move, with all deliberate speed, in the right direction?

The ocean community has defined various short-term strategies: mitigation, for example – the direct tactical response to certain problems to negate or neutralize their effect. Adaptation is a second approach, one for which there is some logic, but which, nonetheless, compromises response by settling for the existing circumstance as the new normal, accommodating the lesser condition, lowering the bar, giving in. Elsewhere, I have argued for a third response: invention, the pro-active, creative approach that applies present and future technology, financial incentive, and political action to new ideas, new instruments, new behaviors, new values. But this, too, may not be totally sufficient in that, while it presents novel strategies and applications, it may not have the underlying power to shift people's values.

Value changes are the most ephemeral, most important aspects of the discussion. We live in a society that has been defined by historical events and cultural traditions that are hard to deny, an evolution of behaviors based on religious assumptions, economic theories, and, sometimes, tumultuous governance. The world wants to be organized around a collective desire for political order, growth as a path to well-being, and capital defined first by the exploitation of natural resources and their transformation through manufacture, and second, more recently, by scientific innovation and technology. We debate the dichotomies – guns versus butter, free market versus managed economy, consumption versus conservation – and the arguments reach a point now when we suffer from ideological adamancy, class differentiation, and political paralysis. It seems a critical moment. We can continue to suffer failed consensus and social stasis; we can experience decline to collapse, chaos, even revolution; or, we can regain our capacity for civilization by facing our problems, accepting the alternatives, and moving forward and away from default and defeat.

Sustainability is a new value that is advanced to this end. It accepts the finite capacity of Nature to support a burgeoning world population. It proposes new behaviors predicated on this knowledge: that we will only exploit resources to an extent that allows for their renewal and sustainability over time We will incentivize and promote this new value system through financial tools, price structures, legislative action, regulatory enforcement, and cooperative action. We will stop taking it all, acting unilaterally and independently for unlimited profit, and will reorganize ourselves to maintain and nurture the natural systems that have sustained us, and will continue to sustain us, even as we grow in numbers, and we choose to make it so.

But, what more can we do to convince the population at large that sustainability is an essential value for our future? Smarter folks than I struggle with this problem. And, clearly, the struggle is necessary to counter those who will not consider or accept even the idea, much less the concomitant action, required to make sustainability succeed. What else is required to convince the body politic that such destructive indifference – by individuals, corporations, and governments – is no longer acceptable?

Let me suggest the concept of reciprocity. This is not a new idea, to be sure; but it might be useful if applied in a new context. Reciprocity is a state of mutual exchange; the categorization of an action by its motivation and consequence in relationship to another. Indigenous peoples have practiced reciprocity as cultural behavior through direct barter and giving of gifts. The cultural anthropologist Claude Levi-Straus identified levels of such exchange – through language, kinship, and economics – as a process that created bonds of social obligation present and future, an idea familiar through the popular notion of the "favor bank," a value on deposit that must be paid back in kind.

What if we accepted the power of reciprocity as a standard of behavior at all levels, in all areas of exchange, with Nature? What if we acknowledged that the land and sea provide us value, not for the taking and exhausting as an entitlement, but as the giving of a gift, the making of a loan, with a consequent obligation that we pay back that value through complementary behavior, equitable patterns of consumption, and forms of exchange that sustain Nature through accepted future obligation? What if we accept such a reciprocal relationship and system of connection with Nature as our contribution – nay, our obligation – to ourselves, our children, and the public good? Let me offer three illustrative statements.

First: By not taking, we are giving back. If we choose to forego or reduce our consumption of fossil fuels or plastic bags or tuna, we are leaving that value for others, a collective choice that, taken to scale, will extend or conserve that resource at a sustainable level.

Second: By paying a fair price for what we need and use, we are giving back. If we pay for our consumption at a level of true cost – withdraw subsidies for fossil fuels;

reinvest such underwriting in clean technology; price water as the most valuable commodity on earth; include insurance payment for disaster response and reparation from environmental destruction as part of regulatory requirement and permit fees; evaluate government investment projects based on a neutral or positive comparison of public benefit versus private profit; increase taxes and royalties to establish financial disincentives for polluting industries; allocate penalties to support non-polluting alternatives; and many other financial calculations and market applications based on the value added by environmental protection and sustainability outcomes – we demonstrate a full, responsible accountability based on reciprocity.

Third: By acting and applying these values, we are truly giving back. Modify personal, family, and community behaviors in every way possible to affirm these values through action. Become a "sustainability" citizen, a Citizen of the Ocean. Set an example. Sign petitions. Vote. Demonstrate when necessary. Communicate your commitment at every level, and hold others accountable in your daily purchases, your employment, your investments, civic organizations of which you are a member, schools that you attend or have attended, churches that you belong to, recreational activities that you enjoy, and politicians that you support. Communicate. Advocate by example. And amplify your voice by joining other exemplars into a movement of giving back.

Of course, I anticipate the reaction to these ideas: as politically naïve, impractical and impossible, too radical, too whatever – all the predictable response by those who don't care, whose personal benefit is threatened, or who are afraid of any change. But, in fact, it is their behavior that exemplifies these accusations: the simplistic political recalcitrance that sustains the status quo, the impracticality – indeed, impossibility – of sustaining our way of life at present levels of consumption, and the radical inflexibility and fearfulness that have brought governance to a standstill. What I am describing is a democratic process and expression of popular will, based not on narrow ideology, but on our understanding of the consequences for us all if we fail to act.

Reciprocity makes everyone a winner, everyone a builder, everyone a giver. It is a simple framework that allows us to understand another way of being; how to support, individually and collectively, a shift from our present way that is making us all losers, all destroyers, and all takers until we have nothing left. Is that really what we want for the land, for the ocean, for our children and their future?

Reciprocity. It seems so clear. Think about what the land gives us; what the ocean gives us. Are we not obligated to respond? Let's start giving back.

A GREEN SWAN

I went to a lecture by a psychologist/psychotherapist discussing the social response by individuals and communities to the "global climate emergency" through "transformational resilience," an approach developed "to teach behavioral, cognitive, and relational concepts and practices that can support emotional and interpersonal sustainability through the years of uncertainty and calamity that appear to be in store." As the news of climate consequence burgeons around us, there is no doubt that the real and perceived adversity worldwide can generate concern and anxiety, paralyze individual and collective action, and undermine the mitigation and invention required if we are to react to sustain our future. As these events have unfolded – the violent storms and tsunamis, the rampant fire, the drought desiccating the fields and foods, the waves of desperate climate refugees – we all have every reason to wonder "what will it take" to convince leaders and government, event private industry, that these challenges must be met. What will it take? I ask this all the time, and I never seem to get an answer.

One evocation of what is lost in all this reality is the pastoral image of birds; the doves of peace, free-flying gulls, white swans floating tranquilly in idyllic ponds. The news also reports the true calamity of literally millions of birds – indeed, billions – over the past few decades, lost to changing climate conditions, their migration and feeding patterns interrupted, and their reassuring solace lost to an uncanny silence. Empty landscapes; natural melancholy; soundless angst. What would the world be if there were no more swans?

In my search for an answer, I came across a paper published by the Banque de France, a member of BIS (a large international group of central banks and economists), addressing the implications of climate change. Francois Villeroy de

Galhau, the French bank's Governor, writes in the Foreward: "Climate change poses unprecedented challenges to human societies, and our community of central banks and supervisors cannot consider itself immune…" He concludes, "…the stark reality is that we are all losing the fight against climate change."

The central bankers understand.

Even economists can find power in metaphor. A concept put forward in 2007 by Nassim Nicholas Taleb suggests certain disruptive financial events, named "black swans," with three special characteristics: they are unexpected and rare, wide-ranging and extreme, and explicable only after the fact. Taleb, a Lebanese American, has been a university professor, practitioner of mathematical finance, a hedge fund manager, derivatives trader, and author of provocative books on economics, both theoretical and practical. The metaphor continues to serve with the designation of "green swans," further differentiated from their dark brethren by the prevailing certainty that climate events will continue to materialize in the future; that there is need for ambitious, imperative actions in response; that climate catastrophes are even more serious than systemic financial crises, posing an existential threat to humanity; and that the complexity of challenge and response is of a higher order, with untoward chain reactions and cascade effects associated with both physical and transition risks, generating fundamentally unpredictable environmental, geopolitical, social and economic dynamics. Green swans are new to scientific classification and do not bode well for the future. The authors of the BIS report go on to observe that "this complex collective problem requires coordinating actions among many players, including governments, the private sector, civil society and the international community, and, indeed, central banks…engagement that may include climate mitigation policies such as carbon pricing, the integration of sustainability into financial practices and accounting frameworks, the search for appropriate policy mixes, and the development of new financial mechanisms at the international level." To enact all this as a climate defense will require formidable "transformational resilience" and significant – perhaps not yet known – behavioral, cognitive, and relational concepts and practices in revolutionary response.

I suggest that we are now in the midst of our first major global "green swan" event.

Consider the worldwide impact of the coronavirus outbreak identified in the Hubei Province, Wuhan region of China – a respiratory disease, like the SARs and MERS epidemics previously, that expresses symptoms resembling the common cold, but can lead rapidly to serious pneumonia and death, spread by human interaction and contact through air, water, and touch. Is this disease climate related? It appears to have originated in the poor hygenic conditions of a seafood market. Perhaps first distributed by bats? How will we know? Will we know in time? Public health officials in China and elsewhere have reacted with an urgency that suggests possible pandemic. International response has been dramatic: literally tens of millions of people confined to their homes, cases isolated, quarantine centers identified or built new, regional and international movement by ground, plane, and ship constricted or canceled, screening at border crossings and major points of entry worldwide. There is a new sense of urgency now, as if we already know that we are dealing with dimension and consequence heretofore unimaginable.

And then consider the financial implications of this possibly pandemic disruption in a wholly integrated global economy. Consider the cessation of manufacture, supply chain interruption; factories closed, workers confined, revenues lost, and sudden uncertainty, even panic, in world markets at all-time highs. The massive collective response signals the significance of circumstance outside modern experience – the realization that without equally massive resilience and immediate transformational change, the world economy and all its social and political inter-connections will be overwhelmed by a vengeful bird. Are we ready for the innocence and the anger of a green swan? Is that what it will take?

As of this writing, there are more than 55 million Coronavirus cases worldwide; 11 million in the United States, and upwards of 250,000 deaths, and there are surely more tragic waves to come.

REFLECTION

THE PRIVILEGE OF NATURE

I sailed for three weeks along the coast of Nova Scotia and back. It was not a mighty ocean passage, although it was out of sight of land often, and subject to changes in weather and wind that provided at least a suggestion of what it might have been to have made such voyages in the past, without a modern vessel and all the navigational technology that fixes your place in ocean space and time.

The time was long enough to forget about work left ashore, to enjoy a truly relaxing emptiness of mind, and not to worry about work to come until I was a few days back and realized there were things that needed doing and I'd best get started.

We anchored in remote coves with no houses ashore and no other boats nearby. There was a profound silence – at least, an absence of the kinds of sound we hear in urban and suburban places. There were all sorts of noises – the changing velocities of the wind, the waves ashore on mud banks or granite rocks, the calls of the various birds, the loon of course, but others – not such novel hearings, but different, isolated, evocative nonetheless.

What struck me in those places was the extraordinary privilege of being there: of being distant, remote, private, undisturbed by the hard sounds of modern living. There was not even the tap-tap sound of keyboards and hand devices, sending forth assertions of where we were, or what we were doing. The choice was to write observations down or to make a mental note of the feeling, not with words, necessarily, but remembered sentiments or observations.

The privilege of being in Nature: on land, the last great luxury is privacy. People pay millions for the illusion of being separate, behind walls, in protected communities. "Natural experience" is a private garden, city park, a run or bike along a designated path. We cram into the national parks; we bring Nature home as plants and flowers grown industrially far away, as brochures for eco-travels to packaged encounters, as books and films that provide projections of Nature, glorious to imagine, but not real. We bemoan the loss of nature, contact with Nature, even as we lament its spoilage and decline.

An ocean experience is different: sensuously, psychologically, and evocatively. The wildness, even of a crowded beach, is evident in light and motion and feeling. The ocean is empty and full simultaneously; it scares us and fills our hearts with joy. It is vast and empty, as close as a tide pool, or deep and fulsome, filled with marine creatures.

The privilege I felt in my ocean place was stunning and overwhelming. I felt guilt and exultation. I was there – so many were not, and would never see or know what I did there. How could I share my feeling? How could I act more effectively to protect such places for others to discover? How could I resist the terrifying and relentless forces of consumption, of extraction and exploitation of nature, of the pollution and destruction of Nature? These challenges quietly crystallized into a noisy conclusion and high resolve.

In that distant anchorage, isolation and privilege were transformed into renewed commitment for engagement and action for the protection and understanding of Nature as the primeval force for self-improvement, community development, and social advancement, as a universal, democratic, equitable force for everyone. My commitment was to the ocean. My privilege became my obligation.

A SELF-HEALING PLACE
We have long perceived the ocean as a self-healing place. Fair enough, given for centuries its implacable capacity to receive and assimilate the detritus of our living ashore. We have deposited into it our waste of every kind, in growing, exponential, volume. We have not hesitated, deliberately or accidentally, to dispose therein our sewage, garbage, toxic manufacturing by-product, chemical effluent, lost ships, even our dead. It was not so long ago that offensive pipes from somewhere inland protruded into the sea to release foul, incomprehensible streams of poison, and we gave this, if we were even aware, no second thought. Nor did we consider that the towers of our power plants or the tailpipes of our cars might release invisible emissions into the air, that would not waft innocently above the land, but dissolve into water as acid, concentrated enough to change the basic pH of streams and lakes – even the ocean itself – to interrupt the food chain or suffocate every living thing therein.

The ocean is so vast; what difference could it make? How could these incremental bits and pieces of human activity ever add up to such an outcome? And, if so, what ultimate effect could be imagined that would dissuade us from the benefits of the industrial revolution, technological advancement, and improved quality of life? As with the raw materials we extracted from the land for this extraordinary human progress, how could the ocean, so enormous in its extent, ever be finite or taxed to its limit?

Our assumption was that Nature existed only to meet our needs. We were to apply our imagination and innovation to the transformation of natural resources into energy, implements, systems, and wealth – in sum, to feed, shelter, and improve our lives in an ever-increasing radius of expectation and well-being. These resources were perceived as infinitely available for us to consume – at first for our basic needs, then for our desires, and then for our entertainment. There was no envisioned limit to fuel, water, or the productivity of the land and sea; so why not take whatever, forever, without hesitation?

To be sure, these are not observations or alarums newly made or sounded by me. We have heard these laments for decades, and we have attempted to deal with some of the effects with regulatory legislation to protect clean air, clean water, and coastal wetlands. Nonetheless, we have proudly dammed and relocated rivers from their natural flow, decapitated mountaintops to be screened, transported, and burned, filled those wetlands, and organized our lives around the automobile – all to sustain a voracious appetite for growth, consumption to feed consumption, a cultural gluttony that has gone mostly unlimited – yes, now even those once well-meaning attempts to limit the demand in the name of conservation and public health are going by the political wayside as a result of diminished supply, increased cost, and the corporate insistence of those who feed on the feeding. But don't worry, never fear, if we need more, we can always find it safely and cleanly and infinitely in the ocean.

That assumption has been severely challenged over the past years – by tsunami, extreme weather, offshore accidents of our making, and evidence of collapsing fish stocks and diminished biodiversity. Ocean research continues to reveal what have been the invisible impacts of these actions. In my doctor's office, I was looking at a poster alerting patients to the dangers of eating certain fish – different species such as tuna, shark, swordfish, et cetera – containing critical amounts of mercury and other chemicals specifically inimical to the health of pregnant women, among others. Afterwards, at the supermarket counter, were displayed those same fish, purportedly better for us than processed foods or meat products chemically enhanced. The swordfish was selling briskly.

Isn't it as obvious as that? The ocean did not protect that fish from the circulating poison; that fish was not protected from relentless market demand; and that consumer was not protected from an unexpected threat to health and life. In that one ubiquitous situation lies evidence of the growing proof that the ocean is no longer a self-healing place.

THINKING LIKE AN ISLAND
Discussing solutions to challenges on land and sea, I often speak of patterns of consumption. We are a society organized around apparently insatiable consumption – of our natural resources, of the products derived from those resources, even of our heroes, who we use up and discard with abandon equal to changing fashion – and it is this drive that has created such stress on our terrestrial and marine environments. Our social needs and financial system enable the extremes: for example, fishing tuna to exhaustion to meet immediate lucrative demand with no concern for limits or the inevitability of extinction.

Some argue this is the evil result of capitalism. Think of it this way: we approve investment in research and development of pharmaceutical products that treat disease; we disapprove of similar investment in such products that compromise the health of our children. It seems to me that the problem lies not so much in the financial system itself, but rather in the investment and consumer decisions and their consequences: either heal our sick, or poison our fields, streams, and ocean. It's all about values.

How, then, do we shift our priorities, change our behaviors, alter our patterns of consumption, make different decisions so as to sustain the resources that remain and assure our future survival? I suggest that we start thinking like an island.

Assume the satellite perspective: look down upon the earth to view an ocean world dotted by islands, be they atolls, nations, or continents. If you now descend and join those island communities, you will discover people whose lives are defined by different limits, different needs, different utilities. Islanders are, by definition, more reliant on things to hand: water locally drawn, food locally raised or harvested from the sea, local skills required to make and fix things for themselves. They are more or less connected to a mainland that may provide fuel, additional supplies, even law enforcement, doctors, and priests, but they know that fog or storm may cancel that connection at any moment and they will be required to fend for themselves. I have no interest in romanticizing island life; it is hard, challenging, often lonely, not always united in politics and beliefs, and forever formed by natural forces.

Nonetheless, these circumstances demand different standards for living. Islanders must focus on first things: on utilitarian needs, not frivolities; on the essential requirements of individuals, families and neighbors. Islanders re-use and re-cycle things; they run machines longer on precious little fuel. They invent and create; islands are good places for artists and makers. They police and govern themselves. They teach and coach children. Islanders choose to limit themselves to the circumference of the land and to the quality of the life so defined by the omnipresent maritime beauty and enduring community they have found and built there. Many times, islanders choose to stay because they reject the way of living on another shore. They are not ocean-bound; with the Internet, they can communicate and exchange goods, services, and ideas worldwide.

What are the characteristic values evident in such places? Independence, self-reliance, practicality, frugality, ingenuity, respect for work, success within limits, cooperation, and community. What if we drew invisible lines through urban places and applied these same values there? What if we looked at our cities, our regions, even our nations, as islands? What if, as citizens, we all start acting like islanders, applying such values individually, locally, and nationally in our purchases, our institutions, our expectations of governance, our life choices? What if we abandon the rigid, mis-valued ideologies that paralyze us, and engage instead in a fulsome exercise of island living? Do we have to wait for our leaders to tell us what to do?

Why can't we do this for ourselves? And do it now?

The global recession, now exacerbated by pandemic, has brought home to nations and individuals alike the painful bankruptcy of systemic over-consumption, driven by credit, as an unsustainable model for the future. Only the most stubborn retro-gressives hold on to the delusion that all will be as it once was. There are signs among some countries and some executives that the application of such values to governance and business development can be a successful, competitive, and profitable way to behave in the world marketplace. There are signs that citizens of nations whose resources have been exploited and consumed, whose destroyed environments can no longer sustain water and food supplies, are demanding – sometimes violently – the attention or replacement of politicians complicit in the old model. There are signs that in certain successful pandemic response – in New Zealand, Taiwan, Iceland, Japan – that insular thinking can serve to protect from us natural threat through shared values, support for sacrificial response, and community determination. There are signs that we are beginning to think and act as if we understand that earth, too, is an island.

WHATEVER FLOATS

Suspended in the supportive water of the ocean, I was thinking of what it means to float, to displace a volume of fluid with my volume of fluid and to be able to relax, think, feel, even move myself gently from one place to another with little or no purpose.

My thoughts turned to whatever floats. There are the small craft, boats, ferries, and ships that ply the ocean in pursuit of transport, trade, or recreation. These were all around me. They were accompanied by other functional manifestations – floats for gear and bait that serve the lobstermen and women on the bay. The vessels come and go, tying up momentarily to off-load catch, on-load bait. The lobsters are stored in blue plastic boxes, often floating within the physical confines of the dock as if the entire enterprise was supported by the fecundity of the local harvest – which, of course, it is.

When you think on it, you can conjure up floating structures everywhere: floating bridges used to detour vehicles while larger bridges are replaced, to serve as causeways between land in shallow waters or wetland margins, to ford rivers in war for tanks and trucks in advance or retreat; floating hotels in floating resorts, floating bars for floating yachtsmen, floating markets for fruits and vegetables, floating restaurants in Hong Kong and elsewhere that might as well be structures on land for all their indifference to the ocean whereupon they float. There are floating cars, tour buses, airplanes, and floating malls called cruise ships, all mimicking land activities unnaturally on water.

Pools are a good place for floating things: those grotesque inflatable animals for the kids to play on, or those floating mattresses for girls to sun on, or those floating lounge chairs, preferably with double cup holders, for the adults to sleep and burn on. There are floating ducks and toy boats in the bath and hot-tubs. There is that wonderful *piscine*, a floating swimming pool on the Seine in the middle of Paris.

There are floating barriers against the onslaught of the harrowing sea. There are floating navigation systems to keep our mariners safe. There are floating research stations, data collection buoys, and scientific observations devices. There are floating oil-rigs. There are floating cranes, construction barges, dry-docks, and deep-ocean drilling platforms. There are floating power plants, floating wind towers, floating hospitals, floating houses, indeed there are dreams floated of floating cities. There are floating islands of plastic junk, seaweed, human waste, and the detritus of tsunami. There are floating containers, lost overboard in storms, that ply the ocean like ghost ships, filled with China-made dreck, modern plunder, the loss of which concerns no one except perhaps the insurance companies or the unfortunate craft that collides with them in the night.

The most astonishing floating thing I have ever seen was a floating stone boat moored in the harbor at Dournanez, France. It was carved from a single block of dark granite, in a dory-like shape, a trim bow and well-wrought stern, with thin-sides that revealed the chisel marks of its maker. A stone boat! How could it possibly float? But there it was, in defiance of logic if not physics. Why would it not sink immediately to the bottom? It had a place for oars and later I saw it rowed as normally and gracefully as if it had been constructed from gossamer wings.

I returned suddenly from my floating dreams, awakened perhaps by the intrusion of cold or doubt. Returned to the safety of shore, however, I realized that I was floating, still -- in a sea of information, relationship, politics, anxiety, misdirection, and change, in an ocean of knowledge, imagination, expectation, contradiction, and community. I was floating alone, in company, in a crowd of friends and family, in a world of strangers, on a planet itself floating in an endless ocean of space. It was a stunning juxta-positional shift, from unconscious to conscious, from quietude to reality, from thoughtlessness to mindfulness, from passive to active and then some.

Who was I now? An ephemeral volume of fluid? A stone boat? A bright idea? A drifting tourist. An aging gentleman obsessed by the ocean's future?

OCEAN LIGHT

I lived for twenty years in New York City, with all the joys and frustrations of a mega-city. It is a place where life moves at a hectic pace, innovation thrives, and people make, and lose, their fortunes. It is an ocean city, but you would hardly know it because its port is mostly distant, and slowly its waterfront has transformed from a vital working place, to a derelict place, to a recreational place where people come to run and walk and socialize, special, I suppose, in a city where socialization is mostly a function of work

That waterfront is a place where residents come for light. I can remember walking in the deep canyons of the city's architectural heights and seeing a shaft of light illuminating the side of a glass façade, breaking through to surprise me, encourage me, that there is that freedom from darkness, from the weight of work or any other oppressing thing that might be on my mind as a city dweller. I was fortunate to work by the river and so perceived that ocean light more often than most, with liberating effect.

Ocean light. It is a different light in many ways. It is light reflected – relentless glare, or refracted fragments, or dull sheen; a mirror of the various filters of passing weather and the sun moving across the sky. Ocean light changes with the wind and tide and motion generated by forces oftentimes originating far away. An earthquake or a ship's wake can generate a shift in light many miles distant. A passing front, a raft of cloud, even the turning of a flock of birds can cause the light to change. The variety of light is an essential element of sea experience.

It seems to me that consciousness of light is not always top of mind. How many of us live in a lightless world? Artists and photographers, for example, live by light, attempting to recreate or capture its presence in a single frame. We learn to appreciate how light falls through a window onto a woman's face, or to admire how light on walls or natural features can transform a realistic cause into an abstract effect. We objectify light, subjectify light, calculate by the speed of light, and celebrate light in our religious beliefs as a force transcendent.

When we want to see something for what it is, we shine the light upon it. When we have a brilliant idea or realization, we have seen the light. When we want to shout for joy, we trip to light fantastic. When we are aligned in time and space, we know lightness of being.

When I left the city for Maine, my greatest concern was darkness. I live on a hill with a view of the ocean with the express purpose of accumulating every last lumen of light from the open summer days or the closing days of winter. I sympathize with folks who claim to suffer from some kind of light disorder, knowing my own need and concern that at some point there might not be enough to see me through. On those days, I will head to the shore to find the light that seems so abundant near to and on the sea.

How to explain this? We have experienced the cycle of light and dark on a daily basis throughout history, and we have expressed this through self-realization in psychology, precept in philosophy, metaphor in literature, symbol in art, archetype in myth, parable in religion, progenitor/synthesizer in science, and regenerative healing treatment in health.

Light in the forest is illusive and mysterious. Light in the desert is harsh and destructive. Light on the mountain is amplified bright. Light on the ocean is dynamic and pure. When you feel dim or dark or down, find an ocean by which to re-create your self in the fulsome and beneficial redemptive light.

LIFE IN A DROP

I received an astonishing photograph taken of a single drop of ocean water at 25 times magnification revealing the random inventory of life contained therein. The accompanying message listed the major identifiable species; evident is the simplicity of these entities and the complexity of their metabolism and their engagement in the larger process of the ocean as global accumulation of biomass and contribution to the health of the planet. What seems at first understated and miniscule reveals what is so amplified and essential about the ocean's engagement with human life and survival. It is as if all the vast ocean is there, alive in a single drop.

What do I see? First, that fish eggs of many types are abundant, suspended as potential contribution to the food chain either as immediate feed for other fish or as future feed for larger predators, including, possibly, ourselves. There are multi-segmented polychetes, marine worms – similar in appearance to land worms – with dozens of tiny hair-like appendages for motion through the water. There are crab larvae, much more fully developed: a quarter of an inch long, delicate, transparent arthropods with visible internal organs, eight legs, pincered claws, and bug eyes with compound lenses that grow more prominent as the crab matures. And there are Copepods, tiny shrimp-like crustaceans, common zooplankton that are the most basic source of protein for countless fish species. These animals are energetic swimmers with a well-developed nervous system that provides active motility to evade capture.

But there is much more: microscopic organisms in enormous number, such as Diatoms, a single-celled algae, encased in a silica cell wall; Chaetognaths, plankton with eyes and teeth and tiny spines that grapple with small plankton for feed, sometimes injecting a paralytic venom; Cyanobacteria, coiled filaments among the most primitive life forms that use sunlight to produce sugar – that's correct, photosynthesis – liberating oxygen into the atmosphere for us to breathe. Diatoms, Chaetognaths, Cyanobacteria – these are little guys with big ideas, part of a bigger system with even bigger consequences for us all. Relevant. Necessary. Vulnerable.

But there is another aspect of the image that is equally impressive: the fantastic beauty, as if a collaboration between artist and scientist – whimsical abstraction mixed with observed illustration, Paul Klee and Charles Darwin working together on a canvas as big as life. Another association comes to mind: maps of the night sky wherein fish eggs are scattered like stars, worms like planets, larvae like constellations, plankton flowing like a milky way, copepods like shooting asteroids, bacteria like the astral light of distant galaxies, there but almost invisible to the eye.

What do we feel when we confront the cosmos? What do we feel when we confront the ocean? Surely, we are humbled, made to feel almost microscopic in the vast fluidity of space and the sea. Surely, we are moved by the beauty of it all, the inherent sense of time and space. We are awed by the infinite scale and appearance of dynamic change. We are restored by the truth of what we feel, an empathetic understanding of the value of this world we live in and of the obligation we have not to destroy it, poison it, deprive it of the many manifestations of vitality it all its forms. Surely, when faced with such a view, whether through a telescope, a microscope, or the naked eye, this life as we see it: in health and wellness of friends, family, community, nations, our world, indeed, life in every drop.

THE SORROWFUL OCEAN

My resolve is to advocate for the ocean through information, educational service, and relentless communications, such as podcast syndicated radio, aggregated video, a digital magazine, a virtual aquarium, newsletters, book publication, online exhibitions, a sharing space for classrooms, a forum of the best new voices with the best new ideas for ocean solutions, and aggressive social media. Each of these tools demonstrate the vast connection of the sea to every aspect of human endeavor; how the ocean nurtures us and will provide for our future.

This requires constant and varied activity, lots of bits and pieces taken together, providing content as wide, deep, and dynamic as the ocean itself.

Sometimes the subject seems so vast and varied that no amount of outreach can do it justice, and, as I see the constantly shifting shape of indifference, frustration abounds. It is useful to review the challenges – the astonishing number of challenges – to the integrity and sustainability of this profound natural resource. Sometimes, it serves to hear the names of our enemies read aloud:

Acid, carbon dioxide. toxic emissions, methane, oil, fertilizers, chemicals, organic pollutants, antibiotics, plastics, micro-beads, invasive species, noise, radioactivity, mining, urban detritus, household garbage, construction debris, over-fishing, illegal fishing, abandoned fishing gear, human waste, impacts of coastal development, war – to name just a few, in no particular order of impact and evil.

How does one come to understand the full implication of aggressive destructive negativity, aligned against a natural resource that is now proving vulnerable to such assault, limiting its ability to dilute and absorb such behavior – indeed, to maintain its resilience and capacity for renewal? Humans have done our worst to despoil the land; are we prepared to destroy the global ocean and all its potential for sustaining us into the future?

I leap to engage those enemies as best I can, with the tools and resources available. Some success can be measured, and is always inspiring – the sharing and connecting on social media, where the responses and engagement that can be counted and interpreted as progress. Through technology, I can reach thousands of strangers all across the world; I can see their names and photographs, hear their comments, and welcome their sharing of our observations on to more family and friends, to new Citizens of the Ocean.

Some days, from my hill in Maine there is a nor'easter storm battering my windows – our small world shut out by white, the bay obscured by a wild weave of horizontal snow. It seems less frenetic than the usual pace: and the calm permits reflection, the quiet enables a return to the ideas and intentions that generated my commitment to the ocean and its heritage some forty years ago. Forgive me this instance of public introspection as I ask myself: have I gotten anywhere at all?

Can the ocean feel? Certainly, the ocean reveals emotion – calm, anger, and, the contrast of snow and light roiled, dark and brooding, even sorrowful as if it knows the seriousness of the sickness within itself.

Most all of us have known a friend or family member with sickness suddenly revealed, and understand, to some degree, the pain, the fear, and the determination of those who insist on survival. I lost a friend to a fast debilitating disease, watched her fight back with a fearsome Yankee determination, and yet, at some critical point along the way, saw her lose grip and fail. It still seems unfathomable to me that she is no longer vital and capable of providing the friendship and goodness I've come to know from her.

What can sorrow teach us? That we might lose the ocean? We could: part by part, a coastal area devoid of oxygen, a reef destroyed by acidification, a fish species taken beyond regeneration by over-harvest and consumption. We have evidence of such things already. Our fresh water, food, energy, health, and security depend on a healthy ocean: thus, we cannot succumb to despair, lest we lose hold, succumb to our indifference and irresponsibility, and abandon our most important system for sustenance and survival.

What can sorrow teach us? That there is no time for sorrow.

When the weather clears, we must look ahead and see that we have what we need, what we treasure, out there in that expanse of water and light. The mission cannot wait.

OCEAN MOVEMENT

We think of the ocean as constantly in motion. Indeed, it is: changing every minute of every day, in every place in reaction to gravitational force, the earth's rotation, tides, currents above and below, rising/falling in the water column, and the extremities of weather.

Is the ocean ever still? I can think of only one instant that exists between interstices of these multiple forces – that point in time when the tide changes, an absence of all dynamics just for a nano-moment when all vectors pause, twice a day, to live in an existential stasis, pure space, motion-less and free. Many of us search for that same experience today in our occupied and pressured lives. We yearn for quiet places, no communications or connections in demand, peace and solace in our time and place where we can pause, empty our bodies and minds of cacophonous intrusions of movement, be quiet, be still, be pure of heart.

Some of us will never find that place. Some of us may drop out, thinking we have found it. Others will transfer, mediate, or otherwise adopt structures that help protect us from ourselves and circumstances. To belabor the ocean metaphor: we are each in our little boat on a tempestuous sea and must survive the storm through knowledge, experience, and luck, and find a still, small place for survival.

I offer these thoughts in the spirit of renewal. One of the most compelling aspects of the ocean is its offer of solace and support. We go to the shore in search of re-creation – whether or not we bathe, build sand castles for our children, or just sit and burn in the sun and salt as a kind elemental purge through the ocean's concentration upon all our senses.

All religions have some connection to water at the core of belief and ritual: baptism, bathing, place for prayer, symbolic opening to providence and transcendence. We renew ourselves by the sea, and we come as close as we can to immersion in Nature, whether or not at the moment when the tide turns. Re-creation/renewal/regeneration – all words that imply a forward look and a valuable exercise in self-advancement.

To belabor the metaphor again, why not think of the stroke of midnight on the last day of the year as one of those existential moments? Don't let the tolling bells, celebratory horns, confetti poppers, shouts of the crowds in the streets or your living room drown the quiet of that transitory instant between past and future of oceanic life.

A final thought: the ocean as a place that is alive with the human spirit. There is irony there. Think of the millions of us who live by the sea for our sustenance and community, of all those lost at sea, of the growing number who request that their mortal remains be scattered at sea. I have chosen the scatter option myself. Recently, in a place alongshore with strong winds and massive waves, I had the thought that my going there in death was not an ending of life but rather a beginning celebration in a place of vitality and constant motion – myself truly lost at sea, immersed in a community of natural life in all shapes and forms and stages of existence that is eternally nurtured by the world ocean.

THE SOUND OF WATER

How many ways do we hear the sound of water? Just to think about it demands a total immersion in sensory memory and anecdotal recall. What was that sound? When was it? Where was it? How do these questions pertain to its articulation, fractured and evocative, but ultimately limited in comparison to the infinite euphony of water?

Think of water as many sounds in one sound: myriad compositions, with ripples and waves as notation of melodies and embellishments. Every performance is unique; the players invisible; the conductor, wind and weather; the orchestra, a system of conveyance that responds to the direction of planetary turning and gravitational force. Think of the earth as a vast concert hall for the appreciation for how we, as individuals and cultures, explore the extent of water and interpret its meaning, overtly, or covertly through our senses to our minds.

But who is the composer? Is there a creator? Every culture has its story of origin, often connected to manifestations of water: the great flood; the drowning; the miraculous survival; the baptism; the burial at sea. We want to explain, attribute the making of the ephemeral and fluid to a hand that might look like our own, as if we are both an expression of the divine and its maker. Water lies at the core of mystery, the miraculous, the appearances that dissolve into the inexplicable and unknowable. There is no definitive answer to who or how, only the certainty of movement.

Think of the sound of water on water: rain on a pond, incoming waves on those receding. This is the percussion, the underlying rhythm of constant motion, the fluid beat of time and change. This is the code we seek to break when we sit by the stream or walk alongshore, looking for answers, reasons, place, and value. That search is universal, not exclusive to any one of us apart from all the others. What would it be if we all found what we look for when we go to the ocean in search of that life in a single drop?

Value beyond value -- a crest of understanding, of spiritual meaning and psychological solace -- might unite the world, as, together, the whales swim long distances north to south, the salmon return home to spawn, the turtle lays her eggs for the next generation to risk life in the sea. If that is so, why would we do anything to put that conjoining medium at risk by consuming it to extinction, or by poisoning it beyond utility, or by failing to conserve and sustain it as key to our survival? As with so many things that shape the human quandary, it makes no sense.

What would it mean if there were no water? What if all the rain is acid, the wells are exhausted, and the aquifers finally run dry? What if we pollute and consume withou limit? What if changing climate and increasing temperatures create conditions that so erode our industrial, agricultural, sanitation, and urban systems that society is compromised toward chaos? Think about that future as drought, and drought as silence, and silence as the expression of emptiness. Who are we, then, without vitality, movement, aspiration, security, continuity, hope of a future?

The sound of water is the music of life. Without it we are hollow and dry, deaf and dumb, silent and deadly, useless and unworthy. We need it to breathe and grow. We need it to nurture body and soul. We need it to sustain our families and friends, our communities and nation states, our sense of possibility and optimism for a world somehow better, less fraught, more equitable and just. Perhaps it is possible through the magical sound of water.

Go down to where that water flows: as you drink, remember; as you listen, resolve, that such beauty must be shared, and that you are now creator, conductor, and virtuoso performer in the symphonic masterpiece called water.

MOON AND OCEAN
We live by day with the sun illuminating our lives. The sun powers growth and contributes light to the natural processes that nurture our communities and ourselves. But we are reminded sometimes of the destructive power of the sun: it evaporates our fresh water, dries our fields, and foments the wild fires that consume our forests and threaten our life and property. I associate the sun with the circumstances of climate – shifting weather patterns, extreme storms, rising water temperature, acidification, glacial melt, sea level rise, coral bleaching, shifting marine habitat, and so much more.

But what about the moon? From where I once sat on an island watching a spectacular sunset, the full moon rose silently and stealthily behind my back and waited patiently for my attention. The moon does that. While the sun blares and glares and demands, the moon awaits, modestly, demurely, patiently, for notice. Turning around offered another perspective on everything – the view of another waterscape of harbor and horizon and all the implication therein.

The tide was full as well. The ocean was swollen around the rocks and islands, a kind of calm, soundless fecundity that suggested the teeming life within, and an embracing of those edges as opposed to the clash of wave and storm. There was grace there, coherent movement that suggested peace and harmony. And then, there was the uncanny light. We call it surreal in its unexpected clarity, so sharp that we can see moon shadow. The vastness of ocean in that light seems so much greater to me than a sunlit day with its mist and haze. The mystery of the ocean is there to be seen and considered, what is revealed above and what lies below in depth that seems so much deeper and impenetrable than the height of the day-lit sky. One becomes pensive, introspective, melancholy, depressed, if that is your wont, but the murmurs of that water support reflection, perception, solace, cure, even poetry, as antidote to the cacophony and challenge of daily living. There is no need for exclamation or conversation beyond the quiet, appreciative exhalation as an affirmative response to beauty.

As the sun sets, we look for the so-called green spark, the precise moment when we feel the loss of light and rise of darkness. That moment, ungraspable, is an existential measure marking real or psychological coordinates that declare to self and sundry that this, absolutely, is where I am. Not so in moonlight, where things appear ambiguous, profound, less explicable, more unsure. It is perhaps the constant change within the ever-shifting tide, its movement, rise and fall, fall and rise, that forces a continuing calculation and recalculation of one's place along a progress from somewhere to somewhere else, a journey taken without choice, thus best taken willingly and with exuberance.

The tide covers as much as it reveals. The offshore rocks and ledges and the dangers of the treacherous coast are sometimes visible, sometimes not; and so we seek the reassurance of lighthouses, buoys, charts and maps and calculated tables forward for all time to provide the navigational aid and avoidance of danger. But the tide also ebbs and flows with powerful currents that can be used to add power to a passage or even to take us through a dangerous place if we can observe and understand its natural flow. A truly remarkable seaman once showed me how the tide shifting the volume of water around rocks could be used to move through a tight, seemingly impossible passage without either sail or helm. It was a terrifying, but astonishing demonstration of how knowledge, experience, and appreciation of natural systems can be so powerfully and successfully instructive.

So, thanks for the moon, and its ephemeral power and light, which serve to determine and illuminate our thoughts and actions with a unique, inexorable, often-unappreciated force. I feel optimistic and emboldened by these thoughts from my ocean-side communion with the moon.

OCEAN SENSES

The ocean is a place for the senses. Living in the city, amidst the frenzy and the noise the operative function is contra-sensual, a mix of cacophony and nonsense. We are blinded by the lights, desensitized by the feel of the urban space, and deafened by the chaotic mix. We long for the ocean: we move there and vacation there in pursuit of freedom.

There is a massive internal migration in the United States from the heartland to the coast. By mid-century, more than half the population will have moved to the edges, mostly into the density of large urban and suburban regions in search of work and social engagement. We will be running out of shoreline – assumed by wealthy estates, water-dependent and marine-related industries, vestigial public spaces like parks and beaches, and remnants of coastal wetlands that have been protected from the constant pressure of development. There is a terrible irony in the statement that the ocean is the last great wilderness when in fact its access is becoming more and more limited by human settlement, its value compromised by intensity of use. The wheel turns, as the American heartland – once wild, then civilized by the business of agriculture and fossil fuels – is now slowly abandoned again to the wild, as inhabitants move elsewhere.

And then there is the ever-perplexing implication of climate change, extreme weather, and sea level rise that will impact coasts and coastal communities in ways already demonstrated by recent hurricanes, floods, resultant erosion and eutrophication of inshore waters.

What, senselessly, will be lost? Here are some things at risk:

Vision: sight and insight, clarity and purity in a changing palette of colors, all spectral possibilities, from light to dark, from deepest blue, to purest white, to furious black as the front rolls through. Depth and dimension: the two-dimensional frame of the ocean view; the three-dimensional depth to the horizon and into the sky and space where there is no limiting shore; the four-dimensional extension of time as history of human achievement connects across the open sea.

Audition: the sound of resonance, the rolling mellifluous rhythm of waves, relentless, changing, rising and falling, reverberating, mixed with the incomparable overlay of wind. Calls and cries of sea birds. Grating of pebbles and shells on the beach. Fine choral harmonies of blowing sand and sea grasses. The poetry of the wind reciting expressive lyrics of solace, lament, fury, and joy.

Gustation: the taste of water and salt, bits of grit and seaweed, of beach fare – chips and vinegar and sandy sandwiches, of shared plates at a family picnic, each a stimulus for association and times passed, the tastes of youth and age, of memories.

Olfaction: the smell of wind, changing with direction, off-shore, in-shore, around the compass, riding in and away to places somewhere else beyond our knowledge, the smell of rain and fog, driftwood fire smoke, sweat and sunscreen, the smells of the past mixed into the present and into intimations of the future.

Sensation: the touch of your companion's hands, your children's embrace, the sun on your skin, the water when you first enter, the cold rising, the decision to slowly immerse or dive right in, the salt in your eyes, the swallowed sea unwelcome in your lungs, the feel of some strange marine creature crawling, swimming by.

Creation: making through our voices the shape of speech inherent in our thoughts as we ponder self, selfishness, selflessness, the secrets and confessions between us, the laughter of playing children, the shouts of exhilaration and defiance, the words of friendship and love, the words we don't have the courage to speak.

All these things aggregate into movement by the sea, a dynamic as temporal as swimming away or dancing on the beach, a search for equilibrium and location in time and space. The ocean is the best therapy; the most powerful place for expression of the human spirit and connection, the source of who we are, what we do, and the meanings therein. We are grateful.

OCEANS OF FAITH

Despite the premise of separation of church and state on which our government is based, religious principles and beliefs today are frequently mentioned and brought to bear on social issues, legislative initiatives, and other actions of governance that impact us all. We hear analysis of the political influence of the so-called religious right; we hear religious principles applied to arguments for or against proposed laws regulations, and even appointments of individuals to key posts in government; we hear individual politicians declare their religious beliefs in speeches as the basis for a position or vote, sometimes in opposition to polls indicating differing beliefs of their constituents.

Their opposition extends to almost every environmental issue: the Environmental Protection Agency, Clean Air Act, the Clean Water Act, climate change legislation, alternative energy, watershed protection, coastal management, fisheries regulation, endangered species protection, national ocean policy, and much more. I have never quite understood this, from my own limited religious understanding and knowledge of the Bible, sensing an inherent, inexplicable, irreconcilable contradiction therein.

The Religious Partnership for the Environment, was founded in 1993 as an association between the US Conference of Catholic Bishops, the National Council of Churches, the Coalition on the Environment and Jewish Life, and the Evangelical Environmental Network provides insight into the interrelationship of water, climate, and ocean and religious doctrine.

On water: "Throughout the Jewish and Christian scriptures, water is perhaps the pre-eminent symbol of life, both spiritual and physical. Abundant, pure water, so necessary for human survival and comfort, manifests divine mercy and healing, and occasions gratitude and rejoicing."

"The lack of clean water is one of the most serious health issues for the poor around the world. Ensuring an adequate supply is an important goal for economic development, and preventing some from contaminating others' drinking water is certainly a demand of environmental justice."

On climate: "Although it seems vast, comparatively speaking the atmosphere forms only the thinnest envelope around the mass of the earth. By introducing a few novel gases into the air, we have thinned the ozone layer that protects life on earth from deadly ultraviolet radiation. By burning fossil fuels such as coal, oil and gas, we have injected harmful pollutants and particles into the air we breathe. Moreover, we have increased the atmosphere's heat-trapping properties, potentially altering earth's climate for generations to come."

On oceans, specifically from the Evangelical perspective: "God's oceans may indeed be vast, but they are not invincible to our behavior. For instance, populations of large predatory fish have been reduced to 10% of pre-industrial levels. Nearly one third of the world's fisheries are being fished at their maximum level."

"Current estimates are that 10% of all coral reefs are degraded beyond recovery. Thirty percent are in critical condition and may die within 10 to 20 years. Sixty percent of the world's coral reefs may die completely by 2050. The destruction of coral reefs is indeed unfortunate, because they harbor more than 25 percent of all known marine fish, as well as a total species diversity containing more phyla than rainforests."

There is much more. But here is their conclusion: "While the current state of God's oceans could tempt us to despair, as Christians we must remember that the One who walked upon the water is ultimately the Lord of Lords, and He has empowered us to care for His waters. As followers of Christ, the protector and Sustainer of all life, we cannot forget His oceans, nor can we think of them as invincible and not in need of our care and protection. That He has reconciled all things is our hope – and what we are called to participate in."

If, indeed, we are called to participate, to care for and protect water and climate and all living things as God's will, why then do we obfuscate and deny the research and science affirming positions quoted here? Why do we act against the interest of human health, economic necessity, and social justice? Why do we invoke scripture and religious belief to act against the very lessons of that scripture and the very essence of those beliefs?

Given this terrible irony, is it not fair to ask those who stand against these interpretations of divine will, who it is, in reality, that they serve?

POPE FRANCIS AND THE OCEAN
In September 2015, Pope Francis completed a triumphal visit to the United States, where he addressed the United Nations, a joint meeting of the US Congress, and other gatherings where Catholics and non-Catholics alike welcomed his message of tolerance, inclusiveness, and social justice. The Pope has been especially clear and vocal about his views of climate change as a real, pervasive, and devastating factor in today's world, and that our understanding and response to the problem is essential to the future survival of all people worldwide.

Laudato Si, his encyclical from March of that year, *On Care of our Common Home*, speaks generally about deep reverence for and the active conservation of Nature as a preeminent perspective of the Catholic Church, but it also speaks very specifically about aspects of the ocean. Here is a selection of direct quotations from the encyclical that constitute a series of warnings, of which we should all be aware.

Concerning Polar Plight: "The melting in the polar ice caps and high altitude plains can lead to dangerous release of methane gas, while the decomposition of frozen organic material can further increase the emission of carbon dioxide."

Concerning Sea Level Rise: "A rise in sea level...can create extremely serious situations, if we consider that a quarter of the world's population lives on the coast or nearby, and that the majority of our megacities are situated in coastal areas."

Concerning Ocean Acidification: "Carbon dioxide pollution increases the acidification of the ocean and compromises the marine food chain. If the present trends continue, this century may witness…an unprecedented destruction of ecosystems, with serious consequences for all of us."

Concerning Ocean-Bound Water Pollution: "Underground water sources in many places are threatened by the pollution in certain mining, farming, and industrial activities, especially in countries lacking adequate regulation or controls. It is not only a question of industrial waste. Detergents and chemical products, commonly used in many places of the world, continue to pour into our rivers, lakes, and seas."

Concerning Overfishing and Seafood By-catch: "Marine life in rivers, lakes, seas, and oceans, which feeds a great part of the world's population, is affected by uncontrolled fishing, leading to a drastic depletion of certain species. Particularly threatened are marine organisms which we tend to overlook, like some forms of plankton; they represent a significant element in the ocean food chain, and species used for our food ultimately depend on them."

Concerning Loss of Marine Biodiversity: "In tropical and subtropical seas, we find coral reefs comparable to the great forests on dry land, for they shelter approximately a million species, including fish, crabs, mollusks, sponges and algae. Many of the world's coral reefs are already barren or in a state of constant decline… Wetlands converted to cultivated land lose the enormous biodiversity which they formerly hosted. In some coastal areas the disappearance of ecosystems sustained by mangrove swamps is a source of serious concern."

As leader and exemplar, Pope Francis asks us these questions: What makes the ocean different or more important in the larger context of violence and deprivation around us? Why should we focus on it, rather than all the terrible problems on land?

My response is that the ocean transcends the exigencies of the modern life. It represents the future: it exists beyond the present moment or crisis; it is the essential system that implies possibility, portends solution, and offers a way forward that will provide for us, whether or not we believe ourselves to be the creatures of any God. Francis embodies welcome and portrays a scape of comparable openness, offers a non-judgmental embrace, and voices an optimism founded on fundamental moral principles, on what is wrong and what is right. If we are alienated from the land, he suggests, then our reconciliation and redemption must be found elsewhere. Why not immerse ourselves in the nurturing ocean and find solace and a viable future in the provident sea?

HALCYON OCEAN

According to Greek mythology, Alcyone, the daughter of the god of the winds, became so distraught when she learned that her husband had been killed in a shipwreck that she threw herself into the sea and was changed into a kingfisher. As a result, ancient Greeks called such birds *halcyon*, and the myth ensued that these birds built floating nests on the ocean that so moved the wind god that he created a state of breathless quiet on the water that protected the eggs until the fledglings were born. This legend prompted the use of "halcyon" both as a noun, naming a genus of kingfisher, and as an adjective, describing unusual, primordial calm.

Calm can be associated with the ocean – a state desirable as an alternative to chaos. On a trip to Antarctica, there was much discussion of the Drake Passage, a convergence of current and weather from Cape Horn southward, portrayed as a collision of wind and wave that wrecked ships and marked its sailors for life as survivors. Our passage both ways crossed a placid sea – birds and dolphins racing alongside, not a hint of any storm to come. I can't say that I was disappointed.

Calm can be also associated with an inner state of being – a neuro-chemical-physical quietude that is a desirable condition that expels and denies the neurotic conditions of our lives and brings us peace of mind and body. Be calm, we say to soldiers under attack, rebels with violent causes. Be calm, we say to our children grappling with their futures; be calm, we say to our parents and friends in illness or the fear of death. Be calm, we say to ourselves en route to Antarctica: "Chill, it's going to be a Drake Lake." And it was.

Why is it that all major religions involve water as an essential place of ritual: baptism, cleansing, purity of purpose and soul? The ocean is a vast reservoir of water to the point of no dimension: its horizon has no meaning; its depth and breadth cannot be perceived, disorienting in space and disconnecting in time. The ocean is in constant movement, and there is no foretelling, even with the best observations, from above and below, that can be certain. A storm can materialize in a sudden shift of pressure; a wind can reach gale force by a minor adjustment of degree; a reef or bar can appear when the charts and satellites assert that for all time there has been nothing there. Clearly, the ocean strikes every chord, each lost in one coherent, resounding tone.

I have a friend, colleague, and fellow ocean advocate, Wallace J. Nichols, who, for years, has given out a simple blue glass marble as a evocation of the Earth from space – presented to any and all, from national presidents to the Dalai Lama to the most secular surfer – literally to thousands who understand the ocean calm, directly or indirectly, through experience, study, and intuition. I have emulated this distribution myself, carrying marbles with me always, as an almost perfect metaphor that I can hold up to the light to release the calm, the fluidity, and the peace of the ocean world in my hand. It connects, it captures and refracts all the available light, and it consistently elicits a quiet understanding between those assembled, even in a crowded elevator, a giant auditorium, and across borders of nations and the boundaries of language. Jay Nichols writes about *blue mind*, what he measures physically in the body, psychologically in the head, and spiritually in the heart – a pervasive state of harmonic blue.

In how many stories, in how many cultures, is there an account of the wife bereft of her fisher husband lost at sea, grieving and regenerating through immersion in such a dynamic, mysterious space? How many floating nests will be accommodated by the ocean, over how many generations? How many fledglings will find the ocean calm to clear their way? Halcyon!

FANTASTIC VOYAGES

The sea has been a tremendous source of storytelling and real-time adventure tales since the beginning of narrative. Almost every culture has its archetypal maritime story – from the Viking *Sagas* to *The Odyssey* to the *Voyages of Sinbad the Sailor*.

There are stories of sea goddesses that have empowered religious cults and artistic expression – Matsu in China for example, or Mami Wata in Africa. There are sea-based entertainments such as Patrick O'Brian's Aubrey-Maturin series, Hergé's *Tintin* or, more recently, David Masiel's *2182kHz* and Carsten Jensen's *We, The Drowned*, both highly recommended stories made more powerfully compelling through their ocean setting.

The great futuristic title, of course, is *20,000 Leagues Under the Sea* by Jules Verne, the story of Professor Pierre Aronax, a marine biologist who, with two colleagues, joins an expedition to track down a mysterious sea monster that has been sighted by various ships and damaged an ocean liner. The monster is, of course, the *Nautilus*, a secret sub-marine vessel of a size never before imagined and sailed by one Captain Nemo, a self-exiled scientist in pursuit of knowledge, independent of the confines of government, politics, and the other restrictions of civilization. Nemo takes Aronax or a fantastic voyage beneath the sea where they visit coral reefs of pure and undiluted beauty, find remnant fleets of ancient wrecks on the ocean floor, and even witness the encrusted architecture of the fabled lost city of Atlantis. These things were, in their time of writing, the essence of myth or the fabrications of wild imagination. In the end, the intrepid explorers escape, while Nemo and Nautilus disappear into the enigma of the Moskstraumen whirlpool off Norway and thence into the annals of literature.

The *Nautilus* pre-visions the submarines we know today, large silent ships with full communities aboard, able to stay submerged for long periods, to visit the bottom of the ocean floor, to transit routinely under polar ice, and to unleash an arsenal of a demonstrative power that not even Verne could invent. Similarly, underwater devices have become important tools for global ocean research, for mapping and data collecting and documenting places and phenomena that have been considered heretofore perfectly inaccessible. There are manned submersibles, deep sea vehicles, and remote-controlled drones that have explored the deepest deep, identified millions of new marine species, and even discovered new ecosystems and new forms of life – now available to a world audience through underwater digital equipment, television, IMAX films, and real-time streaming into classrooms and onto your desktop computer or hand-held device.

But what of future ocean voyages?

Researchers at the Center for Autonomous Systems at Virginia Tech University in the United States are designing and testing new forms of underwater gliders with advanced control technology and neutral buoyancy that will maximize the utility and efficiency of these devices as key tools for underwater exploration in unexpected places. One fantastic application might send such a glider in the opposite direction, into space, to the three moons of Jupiter, thought by many scientists today as a possible location for the discovery of extraterrestrial life.

There is much additional speculative research. Various proposals have been put forward to explore these planets in elliptical orbit some 628 to 928 million kilometers from Earth. One such called for nuclear-powered "cyro-bots" that would melt their way through outer ice layer to release "hydro-bots," autonomous underwater gliders possibly built on the work of the Virginia Tech center and others. In 2012, the European Space Agency selected an orbiter probe expedition to be launched in 2022 in an Ariane 5 rocket to orbit and maneuver around Jupiter and her moons, arriving in 2030 to investigate the subsurface water reservoirs; to conduct topographical, geological and compositional mapping of the surfaces; to study of the physical properties of the icy crusts; and to characterize of the internal mass distribution, dynamics and evolution of the interiors. The focus will be "on the chemistry essential to life…".

CONRAD AND THE SEA

Many of literature's great classics are set on the ocean, where Nature's beauty and force place humans in a context of survival, of skills put to the test, of confrontation with great questions, and moral quandaries that have proved prescient over time to universal human experience. Students of western literature are aware of *The Odyssey* and *Moby Dick* as powerful, familiar examples. An amazing 1,000-page anthology of great sea stories, edited by H.M. Tomlinson, published in 1937, is a collection of sea stories arranged by setting such as: Ancient Greece, Ancient Rome, Arabia, Persia, Celtic Literature, Great Britain, Canada, Australia, United States, France, Italy, Spain, Portugal, Belgium, Holland, Germany, Poland, Finland, Iceland, Norway, Sweden, Denmark, and Japan. The narrative of the sea knows no bounds.

Perhaps the greatest such author was Joseph Conrad, whose works include *Lord Jim, Heart of Darkness, Typhoon, Nostromo, The Shadow Line, The Secret Sharer*, and other novels and stories set at sea and along the shore. His most direct, but not so well-known book on the ocean is entitled *The Mirror of the Sea*, originally published in 1906. Describing his purpose in *The Mirror of the Sea*, Conrad writes, "I have attempted here to lay bare the unreserved of a last hour's confession the terms of my relation with the sea, beginning mysteriously, like any great passion the inscrutable Gods send to mortals…"

The prose, as always, is precise, evocative, and dimensional. Here is Conrad writing about the anchor: "For a ship with her sails furled on her squared yards, and reflected from truck to waterline in the smooth gleaming sheet of a landlocked harbor, seems, indeed, to a seaman's eye the most perfect picture of slumbering repose. The getting of your anchor was a noisy operation on board a merchant ship of yesterday – an inspiring, joyous noise, as if, with the emblem of hope, the ship's company expected to drag up out of the depths, each man all his personal hopes into the reach of a securing hand – the hope of home, the hope of rest, of liberty, of dissipation, of hard pleasure, following the hard endurance of many days between sky and water."

Here is Conrad on weather: "The olive hue of hurricane clouds presents an aspect peculiarly appalling. The inky wragged wrack, flying before a nor'west wind, makes you dizzy with its headlong speed that depicts the rush of invisible air. A hard sou'wester startles you with its close horizon and its low grey sky, as if the world were a dungeon wherein there is no rest for body or soul."

And here is one of my favorites passages, on work and skill: "Now, the moral side of an industry, productive or unproductive, the redeeming and ideal aspect of this bread-winning, is the attainment and preservation of the highest possible skill on the part of the craftsmen. Such skill, the skill of technique, is more than honesty, it is something wider, embracing honesty and grace and rule in an elevated and clear sentiment, not altogether utilitarian, which may be called the honor of labor. It is made up of accumulated tradition, kept alive by individual pride, rendered exact by professional opinion, and, like the higher arts, it is spurred on and sustained by discriminating praise. This is why the attainment of proficiency, the pushing of your skill with attention to the most delicate shades of excellence, is a matter of vital concern. Efficiency of a practically flawless kind may be reached naturally in the struggle for bread. But there is something beyond – a higher point, a subtle and unmistakable touch of love and pride beyond mere skill, almost an inspiration which gives to all work that finish...which is art."

Finally, Conrad's observation as relates to our reflections here: "Water is friendly to man. The ocean, a part of Nature farthest removed in the unchangeableness and majesty of its might from the spirit of mankind, has ever been a friend to the enterprising nations of the earth. And of all the elements this the one to which men have always been prone to trust themselves, as if its immensity held a reward as vast as itself."

LOST

Several years ago, I visited Ireland with my son, a musician, and one day we ventured to a small coastal village in search of the grave of a famous Irish traditional singer whose voice and repertoire had shaped my son's first music in a fundamental way. At the local pub, we learned there were five graveyards in the area and we visited them all in our search to pay homage, a lovely walk alongshore looking out over the sea that seemed as much of the place as was the land itself. We found the stone, and, while my son placed a guitar pick in the ground as a respectful tribute, I observed the other stones there, canted by wind and encrusted by the salt air, almost all of which were the final resting places for fishermen, each marked with name, date, and the phrase "lost at sea."

Ironically, all the stones were facing inland, as if the mourners had insisted that this final resting place must turn its back on what took those lives – and so many others – from a community that fished more than it farmed. By so doing, the community lost generations of husbands, sons, and brothers to a cold, hard, dangerous, and unforgiving ocean.

Work on or by the sea is challenged by extremes of weather, wave, wind, and dynamic forces that can equal the wrath of God. Human responses, even in today's

most sophisticated technical and engineered world, are limited by the shape and
strength of the boat, the durability of the gear, the uncertain availability of the catch,
and the weaknesses of the human body and spirit. The graves in that old cemetery
are not unusual; indeed, they can be found worldwide, along every coast shaped by
the realities of maritime culture.

And then, there are the unmarked graves of men swept overboard, or died and
committed to the ocean as their final port of call – without memorial – how many
thousands of these are there, dissolved in history, forgotten?

I come from the heartland of the United States and did not see the ocean until I was
eighteen, when my father took me to Gloucester, Massachusetts, a town that has
relied on fishing as its primary source of sustenance and survival since its founding.
A famous statue stands there: a fisherman looking out to sea. The local churches have
stained glass windows commemorating over 4,000 captains and crew lost at sea since
the 19th century. The village houses along the Atlantic shore are known for their
widows' walks – on-the-roof look-outs from which wives and mothers scanned the
horizon for the returning sails of whaling ships, absent for years at a time, sometimes
bringing home sperm-oil and ambergris fortune, oft-times bringing nothing but
sadness and loss.

Every major fishing port or coastal city will have its fisherman's memorial, its
monument to lost seamen, its maritime museum documenting the full array of goods
and services that contributed so substantially to the early history of the place – not
just the fishing, but the boat-building and merchant trade, immigration, emigration,
associated international commerce, and the exchange of ideas. Typically, these
monuments will stand at the heart of the old port, in the nearby shipyards, or in the
old warehouses, markets and exchanges, in the sailor-town neighborhoods that were
the physical center and socio-economic heart of these first urban concentrations – in
natural harbors or at the confluence of rivers with the sea.

Today, more and more people around the world live alongshore – and more are
moving there, to relocate to harbor cities with rich regional histories – where the
waterfront and port facilities are being modernized to accommodate the old – oil

and gas imports, automobiles, and container cargo – with the new – the cruise ship industry, residential development, and recreation. These cities are proud of their revitalized ocean-related historical architecture; brick and iron buildings adapted to 21st century retail and offices, the atmosphere of the narrow, cobbled streets enlivened by brewpubs and restaurants, bike trails and parks. The old fish sheds and docks are mostly gone; the buyers and sellers, product distributors and processors, lobster boats and draggers, displaced and re-located inland to anonymous warehouses serviced by trucks. The loss of the Fulton Fish Market in lower Manhattan in New York and the Tsukijii Market in Tokyo are two of the most egregious examples.

What is left behind? A statue, an empty after-thought of a proud history of ocean enterprise and harvest from the sea? It seems a cruel indifference, to abandon that authenticity, that formative force in the building of community, to permit an insensitive forgetfulness of family, friends, and neighbors gone before, once lost at sea, now lost to memory.

THE OCEAN AND ADVERSITY

I attended *Soul of a Nation – Art in the Age of Black Power* 1963 -1983 at the de Young Museum in San Francisco – an exhibition of art by Black artists during two pivotal decades when issues of race and identity dominated and defined both public and private discourse in the United States. It was a heady time for politics, an explosion of Black voices, and a comparable exposure of Black artists whose visual language expressed the anger and protest against suppression, racism, and injustice. The exhibition was powerful and provocative, art beyond propaganda, palpable outrage and creative declaration that the adversity felt and lived within the black community could be endured no more.

Adversity. It's an odd word: a shape-shifter, ranging from hard luck to hard times, from a difficult set-back to a permanent, oppositional state of being. There were very few African or Asian visitors in the galleries. The audience was people like me who, in truth, have known very little adversity at all. Africans and Asians and Latinos continue to face the situation every day, still, in our country; they don't need to come to an art museum to feel or understand it.

The ocean is a scape for adversity. In and of itself, its dynamics are random and irrational, but, nonetheless, synergistic and inclusive of its forces. When humans intrude, leave the certainty of the known, they step into a world that is contradictory, unpredictable, and unwelcoming to the introduction of a small craft attempting to get from one place to another in an adverse medium. The winds are adverse. The tides are adverse. The waves are adverse. In such a situation, survival demands order, cooperation, knowledge, experience, and the subversion of any fixed terrestrial ideal or social prejudices, any inhibition to getting from here to there. Ship's crews united in the face of adversity or they did not survive. Seamen came from all parts of the world, all races – and still do – unified by proven means of discipline, harmony, cooperative work, and patterns of behavior that overcome adversity, even its most violent expression, without bias, without exclusion, without a necessary integration of strength, skill, determination, and respect for those alongside, aboard.

It would be stupid to say that there was no racism at sea. However, the accounts of accord, shared culture and traditions, and the certainty that no single force can better the collective force of many – no matter what their origin or color of their skin – was an operative paradigm. What has always struck me about sea experience, however limited mine might be, is that the ship is both reality and symbol for education: the captain teaches the mate, the mate teaches the crew, the crew teaches each other, in a continuous curriculum of experience inclusive of what we today call physics, biology, chemistry, engineering, history, politics, sociology, economics, psychology, literature, and art. A ship is a university at sea. What we discover at university is that knowledge is not limited unless access is limited, that race has nothing to do with the ability to study or comprehend even the most complex mathematics or philosophical theories or scientific formulae. Thus, on a ship, as in successful society, opportunity, commitment, and work counter adversity, the entire crew working together toward successful passage through any challenge.

Adversity reigns on a slave ship: an inequitable imposition of one system on another, an involuntary engagement, and a social tyranny with inevitable physical and spiritual distress and disruption. The cargo, racially discriminated against, is subject to the most adverse conditions, dehumanized, commodified, all the aspirations and values of civilization for them abandoned; resultant, discriminatory cultural conditions established and continued on shore; human beings relegated to exclusion by race and to a reality of social injustice. Who would not be angry and outraged and politically motivated to protest and bring such violence to an end?

The lessons of the ocean are not just a metaphor. They are real, and they are being lost as we continue to permit and condone racism on land – contemporary events are a sad continuum with terrible consequence for civility and harmony today. We are building walls. We are separating by origin. We are excluding by race. These are terrestrial behaviors that must not endure. We cannot forget the wisdom of the ocean. We cannot segregate the crew. We must not give in to adversity.

SHADES OF BLUE

Here is a definition of *blue*: "the color of the sky and sea, often associated with depth and stability and symbolic of trust, loyalty, wisdom, confidence, intelligence, faith, truth, and heaven." These represent a profound ascent of meaning.

In environmental circles, "blue" symbolizes a vast other part of Nature, not so well known, and in danger of decline by ignorance and indifference. Various ocean-related projects called Mission Blue, Blue Ventures, Blue Mind, Blue Economy, Blue Ocean Society, Blue Ocean Foundation, Blue Ocean Institute, Blue New Deal, et cetera, all devoted to ocean research, conservation, and public awareness, are led by ardent advocates for a blue ocean future, exist to redress this serious misunderstanding of the fulsomeness of Nature absent knowledge of the freshwater/ocean continuum. This work is important, global, and effective, albeit to the limits of available funding, communications, and political receptivity. Let me honor them and invite your support for each and every one without question.

But I would like to consider *blue* as the noun defined, the singular associations that are whole phenomena in themselves. "Depth," for example, as measured by ocean soundings in which the earth's highest mountains are submerged, has a concrete definition. But deep may have no limit to its value – an infinite dimension that extends beyond our imagined boundaries of observations and experience. To go there is to explore without inhibition by either mind or body. "Stability" is another unexpected meaning. The ocean is considered a place of constant movement – a dynamic of tide, current, wave, weather, transportation, war, exchange, and other forms of human intervention. But, within, below, there may be a stasis of invisible systems, in the darkness, unseen, certain, nurturing, a place with the quietude of the womb, a place we all once knew but can't remember.

Pure Nature, then, as in the deep sea, suggests that in the noun there is a place beyond the symbolic, a scape for trust, loyalty, wisdom, for confidence and intelligence, for faith and truth. These terms have bearing, as values, on human behavior. When we mistrust, or are disloyal, or are faithless, we deny the truth of relationship between our selves and the environment that sustains us. Denial renders us lost and vulnerable to the surface, to the seductive, unnatural aspects of human society like excess, greed, class and ethnic division, inequity, and injustice. Does our behavior, knowing and selfish, merit any outcome but that, in our dark place, we drown?

It is our natural predilection to survive. At the bottom, we look upwards and see an ascending path of light, upward from death and emptiness to pass through stages of meaning, shades of blue, toward redemption. We return to essential values so cruelly corrupted and denied to restore what we call civilization. Call it a passage to heaven, out of the ocean to the heaven that is earth, both land and sea. Our most fundamental freedom is to choose. Let's move beyond blue as an adjective, even as a noun; let's express blue as a force that drives transformation, regeneration, and renaissance. Blue will set us free.

OCEANIC FEELING

In my reading, I came across the phrase "oceanic feeling" – apparently mentioned by Romain Rolland, recipient of the 1915 Nobel Prize for Literature, in a letter to Sigmund Freud – regarding a spontaneous religious feeling, the simple and direct fact of awareness of the "eternal" without perceptible limits. Rolland was considering the example of Ramakrishna and other mystics of the early part of the 20th century.

Freud's response and explanation defines this state as a "primitive ego-feeling," a condition that exists in infants prior to the cessation of breast-feeding – that point at which, he asserts, the ego is created as an expression of an independent "self"; a oneness with the world or a limitlessness that is simply a description of the feeling by the infant before it learns, by separation from its mother, that there are other persons in the world. I think I have it clear. This was a very disconcerting revelation for me, who (at the risk of over-sharing) was informed decades ago by no less an authority than my mother, that I was never breast-fed; thus, per Freud, have I remained for all the ensuing years in a state of pure, independent ego, oblivious to others? Does this explain everything? Remind me not to consult a Freudian to find out.

I have "oceanic feeling" every time I experience the ocean, regardless of place or condition. It is as close to purity as I expect ever to come. I am transfixed: by the light, the motion, the smell, the sound, and all the other sensations of body and mind that the ocean inspires in me consistently and profoundly on every occasion. Is it ecstatic? Sometimes. Frightening? Frequently. As profound and joyful an identification of spirit and Nature as I know? Always.

This idea came home to me both emotionally and intellectually when I visited Reynisfjara, a world-famous black-sand beach on the south coast of Iceland, just beside the small fishing village of Vík í Mýrdal. The place is unique and almost beyond description in its beauty. The approach is along a path through secretive dunes with the roar of waves announcing something very dramatic to come. The tan sand turns to grey, then to black – a coarse ground that is both dark and light, tessellated, basalt and quartz in concert, conjoined in an unexpected, anomalous revelation in contradiction to every expectation. Along the way, bits of rusted iron emerge – portions of an anonymous ship, wrecked on that perilous lee shore, relentless waves pounding its humanity to hulk, then pieces, then buried like fragments, lost to an indifferent, hellish place.

But Hell it is not. What emerges with the full scape of the beach is one of the most heavenly beautiful places I have ever seen: glaring metallic light that is both cold and warm, harsh and pure, an arrangement of peaked and cragged rocks offshore, fragmenting and foreboding, refracting the light and bifurcating the rollers. The sound of waves and rattling stones is enormous, percussive, and galvanic. The onshore wind brings bits of wet and sand and disorientation. The birds turn, at once recognizable, and then lost in the light as if dissolved into nothingness by the sun. I had never experienced such a place before. I could neither feel it nor think it adequately. It was simply beyond my imagination: no perceptible limits. Poets try to write of this, artists attempt to paint, and I, neither, will surely fail here, too. Transcendence does not bend easy to words, or pictures, or pyscho-analytical theories. What could I do before such power? Admit to a God? That was not the outcome. But what was?

At Reynisfiara, I was standing, of course, on the penultimate edge. It was the dividing, and unifying line between aqua and terra. It was a glorious manifestation of Nature, and a celebration of self – mine, yours, and others – as distillate and individual as it gets, as dissolved and communal as it can be. There was no hate there, no evil, no anger, no greed, no alienating other. It became clear to me that the ocean was, and remains, the expression of all that is incorruptible and good in this world – pure and simple – and it was my obligation to protect it. I was to presume to be a voice for its condition, its meaning, its understanding, its fecundity, and its universal and egalitarian contribution to the health and welfare of every person on land forevermore. Grandiose ambition? Perhaps. Achievable? Probably not. But that was, and remains, the outcome. It became, then and there, my responsibility, to the very extent of my self, to share the ocean and all its meanings with all who might listen, who might join me, indeed, in transcendent feeling for all the ocean's implications for the best of our selves and for our human survival.

CONFLUENCE

I read somewhere that the ocean is the confluence of 1,000 rivers. *Confluence*: coming together, a weaving of strands – of hemp for rope to haul and lift, as lengths of wire for cable to hold bridges between two shores. There is an entwining of material and force inherent in ocean circulation that begins at the mountain-top and descends from glaciers and springs to those 1,000 rivers through watershed to wetland, from crest to coast, to then mix as energy and exchange, as a living entity from which value may be extracted and transformed by human intervention.

We must understand this dynamic system as both natural and social, political and inclusive. When we do, we enter and move with the flow – efficient transport of everything from force and food, and, today, pollutants and poisons.

The Galapagos Islands became a magnificent concentration of biodiversity as a result of such currents. That wealth is threatened by foul chemicals and toxins efficiently distributed as illegal, unregulated discharge from industry and human excess far away.

There is this notion that the ocean, by virtue of its vast extent and volume, can encompass and dilute such poisons and so it is fine that we dump sewerage there, or fracking residue, or obsolete ships, or nuclear waste, or plastic, plastic, plastic. That has been proven wrong and wrong-headed. The plume of radio-active water from the Takeshima tsunami accident in Japan extended to the west coast of the United States in a few weeks. The toxic dust from mining in Australia finds its way to deposit as far away as onto Antarctic ice in just a few weeks more.

And the circulation goes in several ways, not just in a circular oceanic gyre, but also up into the atmosphere where different currents distribute in contrapuntal ways, and down into the water column to the seabed where marine communities are disrupted by vertical circulation into sediment unreachable by the human hand. "The sea connects all things" is more than a glib statement; rather, it is a fundamental, determining fact.

Culture can be exchanged by the same forces. The most compelling example is slavery, the involuntary emigration of African people in massive number from home to another land, to tyranny, exploitation, and lasting racial bias, violence, lynching, and exclusion from integrated society and opportunity. That this transit of human life brought with it an astonishing contribution to cultural life is sometimes recognized – mostly forgotten – in the social maelstrom of race relations. Without Africa, America would have no soul – not just soul as music that has transformed our world but also as a manifestation of community that is at once protective and redeeming.

For chattel slaves or refugees from modern tyranny, the ocean has been, too, a mixing medium. So many died, and continue to die, in what might have been an exercise of freedom and opportunity. Our welcome was not equitable, moral, or meaningful. Plantations or camps. Masters or violent police. We live in the aftermath of bias; it is on our conscience; it is an outcome of injustice that must be reversed.

The ocean is a great equalizer. It is prejudiced against all who dare; it is sustaining to all who care to live equitably within its fluid boundaries. It changes all the time, as does our history, but survival at sea was, and remains, an exercise of intent and skill, a resolve to adapt and cooperate against challenges that tax experience and sometimes defy imagination. Indeed, those who crew ships are themselves confluential: of mixed origins and race, religions, political opinions, ambitions, and aspirations. The ocean is isolating as a purely natural place, but it is more truly a scape for human inter-action and cooperative endeavor. To be successful in such a medium demands respect, collaboration, agreement, equity, reciprocity, and love. There is realism and wisdom there. And we should pay attention.

Can we learn from this? Can we learn from the circumstance we face today: the perversity of pandemic and prejudice? Can we let the ocean teach us? Can we listen? Can we change? Can we understand that community, on land or sea, is about coming together, living together in welcome and peace? In a global confluence defined by the unity of 1,000 rivers.

MAKING WAVES: FROM NOUN TO VERB
In my Introduction, I ask that we consider how to shift from one state of mind to another: in fact, to will an act of transformation that converts nouns to verbs. Think of a noun as an all-encompassing wholeness, the inclusion of facts and feelings into a precise definition of shifting shape, content, perspective, and substance. There is meaning there, contained in a fulsome perimeter of understanding. I think of nouns as tide pools, tranquil, self-contained communities, busy but internal, surrounded by the imminence of a rising tide or breaking wave that will submerge its integrity until it is discovered again, in the same place, with the same creatures engaged in their simple cycles of life. Scale up from tide pools to estuaries and lagoons, coves and bays, regional seas and out into the vast ocean, itself the cosmic noun, and you have perceived the totality of oceanic synergy and symbiosis.

Verbs are different. They demand meaning in action. They don't just exist, they regress, they progress, but they always move, must move, in omni-direction, and they require agency to do so. Engaging the power of a verb is to ask that agent to exercise direction, and force: the external wave comes and inundates the tide pool, sweeps it up into the power of the ocean that so impresses and intimidates us all. A wave is a force that demands response, either to resist or to enjoin in a direction as current or undertow or circulation that extends around that 71% of the surface of the Earth. It affects consequence. And when we join that wave, align ourselves with that force, we augment exponentially our power to erode corrupted shores, sink indifferent institutions, and humble all the proudful claims of insufficient greatness. We become wave-makers.

But we also enable the power to feed and heal, and that is my true intent here. The challenge to build our global community of Citizens of the Ocean demands reach and extension beyond the predictable, already converted constituents and to identify the millions of the others who, worldwide, if touched, will allow the wave to wash over them and unite their emotions and their behaviors. For decades environmentalists have attempted to persuade fellow citizens, policy-makers, and governors through science, logic, analysis, and program – and some great successes have been reached – but, today, the staying power of that approach has been found vulnerable, yet again, to the power of indifferent corporations, anonymous power brokers, and those who cannot embrace something other or new. Even as the Covid pandemic spreads, the lobbyists and executives and beneficiaries of the old paradigm take advantage to compromise or contradict those accomplishments by executive order, internal management and budget commitments, and self-serving amendments inserted in legislation the principal purpose of which lies elsewhere.

This insidious and not so subtle corruption questions what was thought to be a long-settled conclusion about the conservation of Nature and its benefit for all mankind. The large non-governmental organizations that have been at the center of those accomplishments seem now paralyzed and disbelieving. They have grown large and awkward, competitive and even complacent, and their funders have not yet held them accountable, or have, by shifting their interest and largesse elsewhere. They represent an ironic reversal; once creative and compelling verbs, they show signs of regression into the passivity of nouns, standing generically for what once was active and is now passive, a coherence of what used to be and is uncertain as to what to become in the radically changed world we live in.

That must not be. That must not endure as an acceptable approach for survival in the 21st century. We must see our actions, or lack thereof, in that dramatic and emotional context. Our own achievements are at stake, but, far more importantly, the lives of our children and their children are suspended on that edge. Don't get emotional, stay cool, be logical, we're told; but that approach has not served us well enough, and so I argue that without emotion, without the passion and determined commitment derived from this "riverine passage," through Confrontation to Connection to Revolution to Reflection, from nouns transformed to verb after verb after verb, we will fail at the margins, at Aqua/Terra, with the future just in sight.

What now? Look for the wave. Catch the ride. Hold fast. Lean Forward. The sea connects all things, and will do so, without end.

FORE/WORD

AQUA / TERRA

FORE / WORD

As a contrarian, it seems natural for me to conclude these reflections with a *Foreward*. As these short essays were all written during the last four years, there is a coincident shaping of opinions and observations by the unique political circumstances of that time. Much of my reaction is to the regressive thinking and actions taken by the leadership of the United States. We all have suffered in various degrees by the uncertainty, even malfeasance of certain policies, withdrawals, and revisions of what was a progressive environmental program worldwide: the Paris Climate Agreement being one, denied, with further regress by executive order and the roll-back of decades of regulatory protections for clean air, water, land and sea—and participation in a worldwide effort to redress actions taken against Nature at the expense of us all.

Today, as of this writing, that seems suddenly to have changed, with the election of a new leadership in the United States with an already demonstrated commitment to restoration of environmental policies, standards, and agreements, and to change and advance toward many of the goals and objectives outlined herein, and more. The pressure drop felt upon affirmation of our democracy and progress envisioned for the future was palpable and inspiring; the sense of anticipation and possibility was equally felt and my sense of opportunity for the realization of perspectives and ideas suggested here grew exponentially and immediately. My commitment to next steps seemed suddenly more than wishful thinking and my intent to propose a BLUEprint for that progress to come was augmented by anticipation and joy. So, today, let's move even beyond nouns and verbs, from words to deeds. Let's now make it so. *Forward.*

ACKNOWLEDGEMENTS

AQUA / TERRA

The "knowledge" in *Acknowledgements* seems never adequately recognized or fully understood. Copy Editors are more than correctors of syntax and grammar; just as Graphic Designers often do more than choose fonts or array art for covers. Friends, as readers, know the delicate resolution involved in suggesting even the most dramatic changes, nurturing the author's psyche through risky water. In my experience, these have always been participant in the process, with certain critical perspective and task, but more so with discerning ear and eye.

Aqua/Terra was first read by a mother/daughter team, Queene and Ferry Foster, whose terse notations signaled more than placement of a dropped comma or errant phrase, indeed raised polite, highly useful questions of order and logic that demanded my attention.

Trisha Badger, Managing Director of the World Ocean Observatory and Producer of World Ocean Radio from which editions many of these short essays are derived, is a wise and joyful co-worker without whom the entire enterprise would surely dissolve into the deracinated *aether* in which we more and more today abide. Her insights, sense of order and design, work ethic, and dedication to mutual ocean purpose and engagement are unique, invaluable, and without limit.

And, finally, my deepest gratitude to my life voyage companion, Mary Barnes, whose empathy and grace may be best understood through the beauty of her art that welcomes you into these pages, these faceted "reflections" on the world ocean, our waterland: *Aqua/Terra.*

All the rest – the wrack and weed, the cliché and dreck, the flotsam, jetsam, and granular bits of plastic, glass, shell, and faceted ideas – are mine.

Peter Neill
Sedgwick, Maine
November 2020